Advanced C Programming Exercises

ISBN: 9798884924918

Table of Contents

Introduction

This book contains advanced C exercises that will be useful in expanding our knowledge of the C language, by mastering pointers, structs, files, sockets, as well as other features.

The exercises in this book were implemented and run using The MS Visual Studio 2022 IDE and the compiler that comes with it. In later examples, where we present OS-specific code, like sockets and threads, we present the solutions for both Windows and Linux (using gcc).

In VS 2022, there is no option to create a C project. For this reason, we will be creating C++ console projects and we will make the following adjustments:

First of all, we should change the source files extension to .c

Then, in the Project Properties dialog we should instruct the C++ compiler to compile the project as a C project. We do this by changing:

C/C++ → Advanced → Compile As → Compile as C Code (/TC)

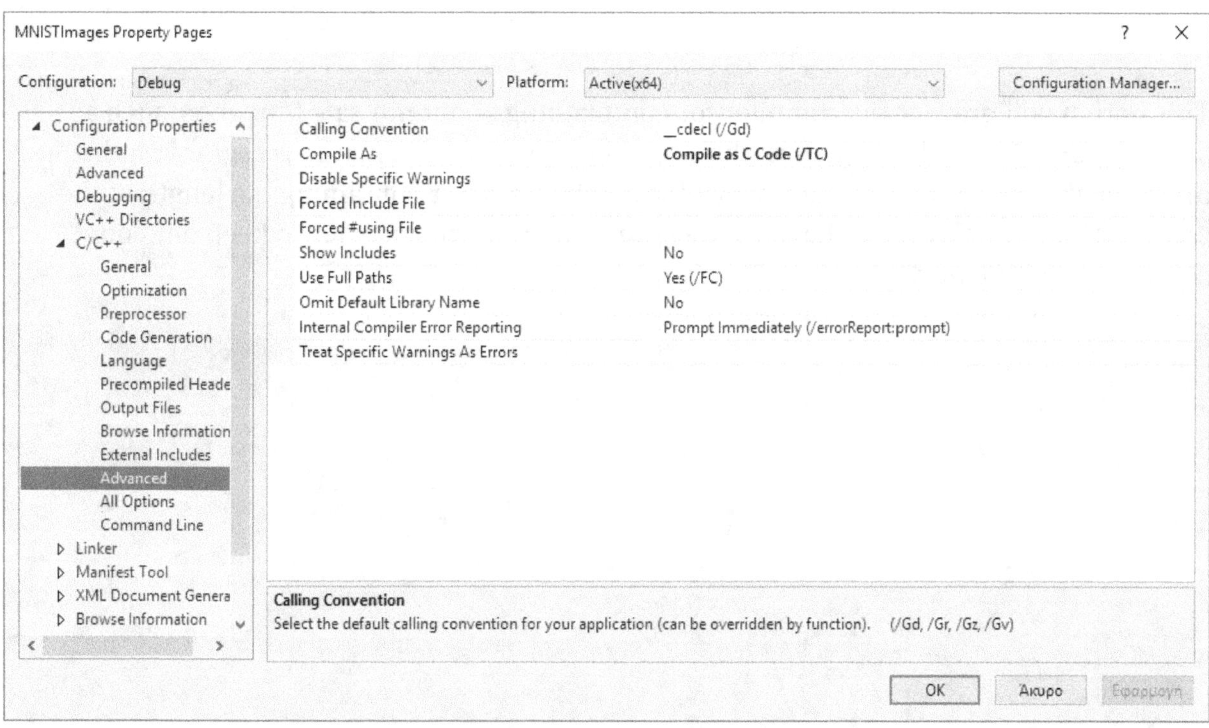

Moreover, we should go to *C/C++ → Preprocessor → Preprocessor Definitions* and add the `_CRT_SECURE_NO_WARNINGS` flag.

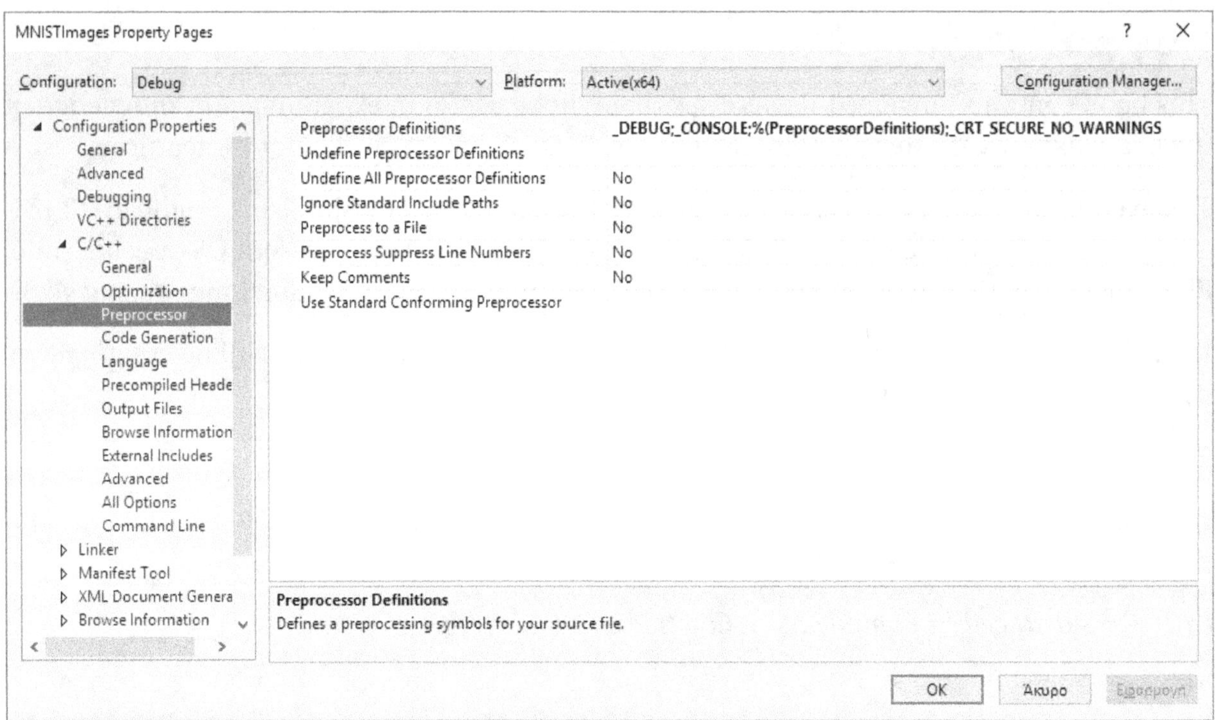

This option will prevent the compiler for complaining about not safe functions, such as `strcpy()`, `scanf()` etc. For instance, the compiler will as us to replace `strcpy()` with the more secure `strcpy_s()` that needs an additional parameter containing the length of the copied string. However, we choose to keep the former form, in order to keep our code compatible with Linux.

1. Movies

Let's create a program that handles movies and their ratings. We need to record the following information on movies:

- Title
- Director
- Duration (in minutes)
- Year of release

We should also define a function that will return the movie's age, based on the current year and the release year.

For each Movie, we should also keep a number of Ratings, ranging from 0 to 5. Moreover, we should supply a function that will calculate the average of the ratings.

In the main function, we should create a movie object, along with some ratings. Then, we should print the details of the movie, as well as the ratings average.

Proposed Solution

We begin with creating the Movie struct:

```c
#include <stdio.h>
#include <time.h>

struct Movie
{
   char name[100];
   int year;
   int duration;
   char director[100];
   int ratings[100];
   int ratingsCount;
};
```

Listing 1-1: movies.c

For the time being we will stick with fixed length arrays for the strings and the ratings. In the next exercise, we will use dynamic arrays. Also note that, in the struct, we keep a counter of the ratings array entries.

Next, we define a function used to add a rating for the movie:

```c
void addRating(struct Movie* movie, int score)
{
   if (score >= 0 && score <= 5)
   {
      if (movie->ratingsCount < 100)
      {
         movie->ratings[movie->ratingsCount] = score;
```

```c
      movie->ratingsCount++;
    }
    else
      printf("Rating space exceeded\n");
  }
  else
    printf("Invalid rating score\n");
}
```


Here, we pass a pointer to a `Movie` object, because we need to modify it. If we failed to use a pointer here, then the changes would be performed on a copy of the original movie object. When the function exits, all changes are lost.

We will use a pointer also in the next function, `getRatingAverage()`:

```c
float getRatingAverage(struct Movie* movie)
{
  float sum = 0.0;
  for (int i = 0; i < movie->ratingsCount; i++)
  {
    sum += movie->ratings[i];
  }

  if (movie->ratingsCount > 0)
    return sum / movie->ratingsCount;
  else
    return 0;
}
```


Here, we don't make any changes in the movie object; we just get information from it to make our calculations. However, it is a good idea to use also here a pointer: in this way a copy of the movie object will not be created, and our program will run a bit faster.

Next, we add a function to calculate the movie's age:

```c
int getAge(struct Movie* movie)
{
  time_t t = time(NULL);
  struct tm tm;
  localtime_s(&tm, &t);
  int current_year = tm.tm_year + 1900;
  return current_year - movie->year;
}
```


In order to get the current year from the system, we use the `<time.h>` library and the `localtime_s()` function. The current date will be entered in the `struct tm` structure.

Finally, we add a display function that prints all the movie's details on the console:

```c
void display(struct Movie* movie)
{
  printf("-------------------------------\n");
  printf("Movie info: \n");
  printf("Name: %s\n", movie->name);
  printf("Release Year: %d (age: %d \n", movie->year, getAge(movie));
  printf("Duration: %d\n", movie->duration);
  printf("Director: %s\n", movie->director);
  printf("Ratings: \n");
  for (int i = 0; i < movie->ratingsCount; i++)
  {
    printf("%d ", movie->ratings[i]);
  }
  printf("\nRatings average: %.1f\n", getRatingAverage(movie));
  printf("-------------------------------\n");
}
```


In the main function, we create a `Movie` object and we test its functionality:

```c
int main()
{
  struct Movie m;

  strcpy(m.name, "Hunger Games");
  m.year = 2012;
  m.duration = 142;
  strcpy(m.director, "Gary Ross");
  m.ratingsCount = 0;

  addRating(&m, 3);
  addRating(&m, 4);
  addRating(&m, 4);
  addRating(&m, 5);

  display(&m);
}
```


Note that we are using `strcpy()` to set the movie and director names. A simple assignment would not be correct.

You can find this project in GitHub:

https://github.com/htset/advanced_c_exercises/tree/master/Movies

2. Movies (refactored)

Let's refactor the Movies program, by introducing a struct to hold the ratings. Moreover, we will dynamically allocate memory for the names' string and the ratings array.

Proposed Solution

We begin with creating the Ratings struct:

```c
#include <stdio.h>
#include <time.h>
#include <stdlib.h>
#include <string.h>

#define MAX_RATINGS 100

struct Ratings
{
  int *ratings;
  int ratingsCount;
};

struct Movie
{
  char *name;
  int year;
  int duration;
  char *director;
  struct Ratings ratings;
};
```

Listing 2-1: movies.c

Note that now we have pointers for the ratings array as well as for the movie and director names.

Next, we define a function to initialize the ratings struct:

```c
void initRatings(struct Ratings* r)
{
  r->ratings = (int*)malloc(MAX_RATINGS * sizeof(int));
  if (r->ratings != NULL) {
    for (int i = 0; i < MAX_RATINGS; i++)
      r->ratings[i] = 0;

    r->ratingsCount = 0;
  }
  else
  {
    printf("array allocation failed!");
    exit(1);
  }
}
```

Listing 2-2: movies.c

Note that we check if the `malloc()` function allocated the required memory for the array. If the returned pointer is `NULL`, then we exit the program.

Next, we define a function for adding a rating to the struct:

```c
void addRating(struct Ratings* r, int score)
{
  if (score >= 0 && score <= 5)
  {
    if (r->ratingsCount < MAX_RATINGS)
    {
      r->ratings[r->ratingsCount] = score;
      r->ratingsCount++;
    }
    else
      printf("Rating space exceeded\n");
  }
  else
    printf("Invalid rating score\n");
}
```

Listing 2-3: movies.c

Now the functions for getting the rating average and for rating display:

```c
float getRatingAverage(struct Ratings* r)
{
  float sum = 0.0;
  for (int i = 0; i < r->ratingsCount; i++)
  {
    sum += r->ratings[i];
  }

  if (r->ratingsCount > 0)
    return sum / r->ratingsCount;
  else
    return 0;
}

void display(struct Ratings* r)
{
  for (int i = 0; i < r->ratingsCount; i++)
  {
    printf("%d ", r->ratings[i]);
  }
}
```

Listing 2-4: movies.c

Now, it is time to add the functions for the movie. First, we define two functions for setting the name of the movie and its director:

```c
void setName(struct Movie* movie, char* _name)
{
  movie->name = (char*)malloc((strlen(_name) + 1));
  if (movie->name != NULL)
    strcpy_s(movie->name, strlen(_name) + 1, _name);
  else
  {
    printf("string allocation failed!");
    exit(1);
  }
}

void setDirector(struct Movie* movie, char* _director)
{
  movie->director = (char*)malloc((strlen(_director) + 1));
  if(movie->director != NULL)
    strcpy_s(movie->director, strlen(_director) + 1, _director);
  else
  {
    printf("string allocation failed!");
    exit(1);
  }
}
```


Note that we allocate one more byte than the length of the original string. This will be used to store the '\0' character for the termination of the string.

Also note that we are using the `strcpy_s()` function to show this function version too. This function gets a third parameter, which is the actual string length that will be copied. If we need to run this code in Linux, we will have to change it back to `strcpy()` with two parameters, the source and destination string.

Next, we define functions for the movie struct that call the respective functions of the ratings struct:

```c
void addRatingToMovie(struct Movie* movie, int score)
{
  addRating(&movie->ratings, score);
}

float getRatingAverageFromMovie(struct Movie* movie)
{
  return getRatingAverage(&movie->ratings);
}
```


In contrast to other languages, like C++, we cannot use the same names as the functions for the rating struct (function overloading). Therefore, we have to provide slightly different names here.

Finally, we add the `getAge()` function and a modified version of the `display()` function:

```c
int getAge(struct Movie* movie)
{
  time_t t = time(NULL);
  struct tm tm;
  localtime_s(&tm, &t);
  int current_year = tm.tm_year + 1900;
  return current_year - movie->year;
}

void displayMovie(struct Movie* movie)
{
  printf("------------------------------\n");
  printf("Movie info: \n");
  printf("Name: %s\n", movie->name);
  printf("Release Year: %d (age: %d \n", movie->year, getAge(movie));
  printf("Duration: %d\n", movie->duration);
  printf("Director: %s\n", movie->director);
  printf("Ratings: \n");
  display(&movie->ratings);
  printf("\nRatings average: %.1f\n", getRatingAverageFromMovie(movie));
  printf("------------------------------\n");
}
```

Listing 2-7: movies.c

In the main function, we create a `Movie` object and we test its functionality:

```c
int main()
{
  struct Movie m;

  setName(&m, "Hunger Games");
  m.year = 2012;
  m.duration = 142;
  setDirector(&m, "Gary Ross");
  initRatings(&m.ratings);

  addRatingToMovie(&m, 3);
  addRatingToMovie(&m, 4);
  addRatingToMovie(&m, 4);
  addRatingToMovie(&m, 5);

  displayMovie(&m);
}
```

Listing 2-8: movies.c

It is important to remember to call the `initRatings()` and the `setName()` and `setDirector()` functions, so that the arrays are allocated some space. Otherwise, the program will likely crash.

You can find this project in GitHub:

https://github.com/htset/advanced_c_exercises/tree/master/Movies2

3. Hospital

In this project, we will create a console application that will manage patients in a hospital.

The hospital consists of clinics (e.g. surgery). We should keep track of the clinic's name and its director's name.

For each patient, we will maintain the following information:

- Patient name and surname
- Year of birth
- The clinic in which the patient has been admitted to
- Room number
- A list of measurements (temperature and measurement date/time)

We should create a function that will return the maximum temperature recorded for a patient. Another function should also display the full information on a patient (and the respective clinic).

In the main function, we should create a number of clinics and patients, as well as add some measurements to each patient. Next, we should be able to change the name of the director of a clinic, as well as move a patient to a new clinic.

Proposed Solution

We begin with the definition of the `Clinic` struct:

```c
#ifndef CLINIC
#define CLINIC

typedef struct
{
  char name[100];
  char director[100];
} Clinic;

void clinic_set_name(Clinic* clinic, char* name);
void clinic_set_director(Clinic* clinic, char* director);
void clinic_display(Clinic* clinic);

#endif // !CLINIC
```

Listing 3-1: clinic.h

The preprocessor directives `#ifndef` and `#endif` are called *include guards* and are used to ensure that the current source file will be included only once in a C program. In this way, we avoid compilation errors that are caused by double inclusion of header files in our project.

The implementation of the `Clinic` functions is as follows:

```c
#include <stdio.h>
#include <string.h>
#include "clinic.h"

void clinic_display(Clinic* clinic)
{
  printf("----Clinic ---- \n");
  printf("Name: %s\n", clinic->name);
  printf("Director: %s\n", clinic->director);
}

void clinic_set_name(Clinic* clinic, char* name)
{
  if(strlen(clinic->name) < 100)
    strcpy_s(clinic->name, strlen(clinic->name)+1, name);
  else
    strcpy_s(clinic->name, 100, name);
}

void clinic_set_director(Clinic* clinic, char* director)
{
  if (strlen(clinic->director) < 100)
    strcpy_s(clinic->director, strlen(clinic->director) + 1, director);
  else
    strcpy_s(clinic->director, 100, director);
}
```

Listing 3-2: clinic.c

We proceed with the definition of the Patient struct:

```c
#include "measurement.h"
#include "clinic.h"
#include "vector.h"

#ifndef PATIENT

typedef struct
{
  char name[100];
  char surname[100];
  int yearOfBirth;
  Clinic* clinic;
  char room[100];
  Vector pm;
} Patient;

void patient_init(Patient*);
void patient_set_name(Patient*, char* name);
void patient_set_surname(Patient*, char* surname);
void patient_set_birthyear(Patient*, int yearOfBirth);
void patient_set_clinic(Patient*, Clinic* clinic);
void patient_set_room(Patient*, char* room);
void patient_insert_measurement(Patient*, float temp, char* date);
float patient_max_temp(Patient*);
```

```c
void patient_display(Patient*);
int getAge(Patient*);

#endif // !PATIENT
```


There are two things worth mentioning here: First of all, the `Patient` object keeps a pointer to a `Clinic` object (instead of containing a `Clinic` object). In this way, we can have more than one Patients pointing to the same `Clinic` object (the patients of the same clinic).

Imagine what would happen if each `Patient` contained its own `Clinic` object: if there was a change in the director of the clinic, then we would have to find and modify all `Clinic` objects (not to mention the waste of memory). This is an example of *Aggregation*: we keep pointers to external objects that are related to the object in question.

The opposite of *Aggregation* is *Composition*: it's when an object contains other objects inside it. This is the case of the Measurements vector. The temperature taken for a patient is strongly connected to the patient and does not make any sense without one. If the patient object is gone, it is OK to delete also the temperature information.

Let's get the definition of the simple `Measurement` struct out of the way:

```c
#ifndef MEAS
#define MEAS

typedef struct
{
  float temp;
  char date[20];
} Measurement;

void measurement_set_date(Measurement*, char*);
void measurement_print(Measurement*);

#endif // !MEAS
```


Note that we opt to use a date string for simplicity reasons. Here is the implementation of these functions:

```c
#include "measurement.h"
#include <stdio.h>
#include <string.h>

void measurement_set_date(Measurement* m, char* date)
{
  if (strlen(m->date) < 20)
    strcpy_s(m->date, strlen(m->date) + 1, date);
  else
    strcpy_s(m->date, 20, date);
```

```c
}

void measurement_print(Measurement* m)
{
   printf("Date: %s, temperature: %.1f\n", m->date, m->temp);
}
```


Vector is custom struct that we create in order to store the Measurement objects. Here is its definition:

```c
#include <stdio.h>
#include <stdlib.h>
#include "measurement.h"

#ifndef VECTOR
#define VECTOR

typedef struct {
   Measurement* data;
   size_t size;
   size_t capacity;
} Vector;

void vector_init(Vector* vec, size_t capacity);
void vector_push_back(Vector* vec, Measurement value);
Measurement vector_at(const Vector* vec, size_t index);
void vector_free(Vector* vec);

#endif // !VECTOR
```


The vector consists of an array that will contain measurement, as well as the capacity and the current size of the vector.

Here is the implementationof the Vector-related functions:

```c
#include "vector.h"

void vector_init(Vector* vec, size_t capacity)
{
   vec->data = (Measurement*)malloc(capacity * sizeof(Measurement));
   if (vec->data == NULL)
   {
      printf("Memory allocation failed\n");
      exit(1);
   }
   vec->size = 0;
   vec->capacity = capacity;
}

void vector_push_back(Vector* vec, Measurement value)
```

```c
{
  if (vec->size >= vec->capacity)
  {
    vec->capacity *= 2;
    vec->data = (Measurement*)realloc(vec->data, vec->capacity *
sizeof(Measurement));
    if (vec->data == NULL)
    {
      printf("Memory allocation failed\n");
      exit(1);
    }
  }
  vec->data[vec->size++] = value;
}

Measurement vector_at(const Vector* vec, size_t index)
{
  if (index >= vec->size)
  {
    printf("Array index out of bounds\n");
    exit(1);
  }
  return vec->data[index];
}

void vector_free(Vector* vec)
{
  free(vec->data);
  vec->data = NULL;
  vec->size = 0;
  vec->capacity = 0;
}
```

Listing 3-7: vector.c

In the `vector_init()` function we allocate space for the array that will contain the measurements inside the `Vector`. Function `vector_push_back()` will enter a measurement in the first empty slot in the array. If the array becomes full, then we increase its capacity with `realloc()`.

Function `vector_at()` gives us a copy of the measurement at the specified index, while `vector_free()` frees the allocated memory.

Now, for the implementation of the `Patient` functions. We begin with the initialization of the measurements vector:

```c
#include <stdio.h>
#include <string.h>
#include <time.h>
#include "patient.h"
#include "measurement.h"

void patient_init(Patient* patient)
```

```c
{
  vector_init(&patient->pm, 10);
}
```


Then, we have functions that set the member variables of the Patient struct:

```c
void patient_set_name(Patient* patient, char* name)
{
  if (strlen(patient->name) < 100)
    strcpy_s(patient->name, strlen(patient->name) + 1, name);
  else
    strcpy_s(patient->name, 100, name);
}

void patient_set_surname(Patient* patient, char* surname)
{
  if (strlen(patient->surname) < 100)
    strcpy_s(patient->surname, strlen(patient->surname) + 1, surname);
  else
    strcpy_s(patient->surname, 100, surname);
}

void patient_set_birthyear(Patient* patient, int yearOfBirth)
{
  patient->yearOfBirth = yearOfBirth;
}

void patient_set_clinic(Patient* patient, Clinic* _clinic)
{
  patient->clinic = _clinic;
}

void patient_set_room(Patient* patient, char* room)
{
  if (strlen(patient->room) < 100)
    strcpy_s(patient->room, strlen(patient->room) + 1, room);
  else
    strcpy_s(patient->room, 100, room);
}
```


Then, we have a function for the insertion of a measurement into the patient's vector.

```c
void patient_insert_measurement(Patient* patient, float temp, char* date)
{
  Measurement m;
  measurement_set_date(&m, date);
  m.temp = temp;

  vector_push_back(&patient->pm, m);
}
```

Next, we implement a display function, as well as the functions to get the maximum recorded temperature and the age of the patient:

```c
float patient_max_temp(Patient* patient)
{
  float maxt = 0.0;
  for (int j = 0; j < patient->pm.size; j++)
  {
    if (vector_at(&patient->pm, j).temp > maxt)
      maxt = vector_at(&patient->pm, j).temp;
  }

  return maxt;
}

void patient_display(Patient* patient)
{
  printf("-----Patient info: ------\n");
  printf("Name: %s %s\n", patient->name, patient->surname);
  printf("Birth year: %d\n", patient->yearOfBirth);
  printf("Room: %s\n", patient->room);
  printf("Measurements: \n");

  for (int j = 0; j < patient->pm.size; j++)
  {
    Measurement m = vector_at(&patient->pm, j);
    measurement_print(&m);
  }

  printf("Max temp: %.1f\n", patient_max_temp(patient));

  if (patient->clinic != NULL)
    clinic_display(patient->clinic);
  else
    printf("No clinic! \n");

}

int getAge(Patient* patient)
{
  time_t t = time(NULL);
  struct tm tm;
  localtime_s(&tm, &t);
  int current_year = tm.tm_year + 1900;
  return current_year - patient->yearOfBirth;
}
```


Finally, in the `main()` function, we define a number of clinics, patients and measurements. Note how we change the name of the Surgery clinic director in one place. Moreover, we can move a patient to another clinic simply by assigning the pointer of a different Clinic object:

```c
#include "patient.h"

int main()
{
  Clinic c1;
  clinic_set_name(&c1, "Surgery");
  clinic_set_director(&c1, "A. Dobbs");

  Clinic c2;
  clinic_set_name(&c2, "Cardiology");
  clinic_set_director(&c2, "B.Smith");

  Patient p1;
  patient_init(&p1);
  patient_set_name(&p1, "John");
  patient_set_surname(&p1, "Doe");
  patient_set_birthyear(&p1, 1970);
  patient_set_clinic(&p1, &c1);
  patient_set_room(&p1, "303");
  patient_insert_measurement(&p1, 37.5, "01/01/2023 00:00");
  patient_insert_measurement(&p1, 38.1, "01/01/2023 06:00");
  patient_insert_measurement(&p1, 37.9, "01/01/2023 09:00");

  Patient p2;
  patient_init(&p2);
  patient_set_name(&p2, "Jane");
  patient_set_surname(&p2, "Doe");
  patient_set_birthyear(&p2, 1985);
  patient_set_clinic(&p2, &c2);
  patient_set_room(&p2, "306");
  patient_insert_measurement(&p2, 36.5, "01/01/2023 00:00");
  patient_insert_measurement(&p2, 38.0, "01/01/2023 06:00");


  patient_set_clinic(&p2, &c1);
  clinic_set_director(&c1, "D. Jones");

  patient_display(&p1);
  patient_display(&p2);
}
```

Listing 3-12: hospital.c

You can find this project in GitHub:

https://github.com/htset/advanced_c_exercises/tree/master/Hospital

4. Package Shipping

Let's create an application that will handle shipping of various types of packages. We will define 3 types of packages, with different formulas to calculate the cost:

- Basic (cost = 2 * weight)
- Advanced (cost = 3 * weight + 2)
- Overnight (cost = 5 * weight + 6)

Moreover, we will create a simple console-based user interface, for the creation, removal and display of packages.

Finally, we will store the packages information into a text file. When the application starts, all saved packages should be loaded into a linked list. When we add a new package, it is inserted into the linked list and the modified list is saved into the text file. The same will happen when we remove a package from the list.

For each package, we will maintain the following information:

- Sender address
- Delivery address
- Package weight
- Send date (a simple string will do)
- Package type
- Cost

Proposed Solution

We begin with the definition of the Package struct:

```c
#include <stdio.h>
#include <stdlib.h>
#include <string.h>

enum PackageType { Basic, Advanced, Overnight };

typedef struct Package
{
  char sender_address[100];
  char delivery_address[100];
  float weight;
  char send_date[20];
  enum PackageType package_type;
  float cost;
  struct Package* next;
} Package;

// head of the linked list
Package* head = NULL;
```

```c
float calculate_cost(struct Package* package);
void load_packages();
void save_packages();
void add_package();
void remove_package();
void view_packages();
```


First, we define the `PackageType` enum that will used to specify the type of the package.

Next, in the `Package` struct, we add the necessary member variables for the description of the package, but we also include a pointer to a `Package` object. This will be used to make the linked list.

Afterwards, we define the linked list header variable and we declare the program's functions that will be implemented later, after the `main()` function. In this exercise, we choose a different style of coding. We put the functions declarations and the `main()` function on top; the implementation will follow next:

```c
int main()
{
  load_packages();

  int choice;
  do
  {
    printf("\n1. Add Package\n2. Remove Package\n3. View Packages\n4. Exit\n");
    printf("Enter your choice: ");
    scanf("%d", &choice);
    getchar();

    switch (choice)
    {
    case 1:
      add_package();
      break;
    case 2:
      remove_package();
      break;
    case 3:
      view_packages();
      break;
    case 4:
      printf("Exiting...\n");
      break;
    default:
      printf("Invalid choice. Please try again.\n");
    }
  } while (choice != 4);

  save_packages();
  return 0;
```

Listing 4-2: package.c

Here we create the dialog with the user. Note the use of the `getchar()` function for the removal of the newline character that remains in the input stream after `scanf()` returns.

We proceed with the definition of the `calculate_cost()` function. The package cost depends on the type of the package asd its weight:

```c
// calculate the cost of a package based on its type and weight
float calculate_cost(struct Package *package)
{
  if (package->package_type == Basic)
  {
    return 2* package->weight;
  }
  else if (package->package_type == Advanced)
  {
    return 3 * package->weight + 2;
  }
  else if (package->package_type == Overnight)
  {
    return 5 * package->weight + 6;
  }
  else
  {
    printf("Error package type! Exiting...");
    exit(1);
  }
}
```

Listing 4-3: package.c

Next, we define the functions that are responsible for loading data from a text file as well as saving back data to it:

```c
void load_packages()
{
  FILE* file = fopen("packages.txt", "r");
  if (file == NULL)
  {
    perror("Packages file not found");
    return;
  }

  char sender_address[100];
  char delivery_address[100];
  float weight;
  char send_date[20];
  enum PackageType package_type;
  float cost;

  while (fgets(sender_address, sizeof(sender_address), file) != NULL)
```

```c
    {
        sender_address[strcspn(sender_address, "\n")] = '\0';
        fgets(delivery_address, sizeof(delivery_address), file);
        delivery_address[strcspn(delivery_address, "\n")] = '\0';
        fscanf(file, "%f\n", &weight);
        fgets(send_date, sizeof(send_date), file);
        send_date[strcspn(send_date, "\n")] = '\0';
        fscanf(file, "%d\n", &package_type);
        fscanf(file, "%f\n", &cost);

        // Create a new package node and add it to the linked list
        Package* new_package = (Package*)malloc(sizeof(Package));
        strcpy(new_package->sender_address, sender_address);
        strcpy(new_package->delivery_address, delivery_address);
        new_package->sender_address[strcspn(new_package->sender_address, "\n")] = '\0';
        new_package->weight = weight;
        strcpy(new_package->send_date, send_date);
        new_package->package_type = package_type;
        new_package->cost = cost;
        new_package->next = head;
        head = new_package;
    }

    fclose(file);
}

void save_packages()
{
    FILE* file = fopen("packages.txt", "w");
    if (file == NULL)
    {
        perror("Error opening file");
        exit(1);
    }

    Package* current = head;
    while (current != NULL)
    {
        fprintf(file, "%s\n%s\n%.2f\n%s\n%d\n%.2f\n",
            current->sender_address, current->delivery_address,
            current->weight, current->send_date, current->package_type, current->cost);
        current = current->next;
    }

    fclose(file);
}
```


We will use a simple format for the text file, where each package field will be written into its own line. Since the sender and delivery address will definitively have spaces, we will not use `fscanf()` to read them from the text file, but instead will go for the `fgets()` option. Moreover, note that we use the newline ('\n') character when we `fscanf()` for the numbers; this will make the trailing newline from the file to be read too.

Here is the code for the addition of a new package:

```c
// add a package to the linked list
void add_package()
{
  Package* new_package = (Package*)malloc(sizeof(Package));

  printf("Enter sender address: ");
  fgets(new_package->sender_address, sizeof(new_package->sender_address), stdin);
  new_package->sender_address[strcspn(new_package->sender_address, "\n")] = '\0';

  printf("Enter delivery address: ");
  fgets(new_package->delivery_address, sizeof(new_package->delivery_address), stdin);
  new_package->delivery_address[strcspn(new_package->delivery_address, "\n")] = '\0';

  printf("Enter weight: ");
  scanf("%f", &new_package->weight);
  getchar();

  printf("Enter send date: ");
  fgets(new_package->send_date, sizeof(new_package->send_date), stdin);
  new_package->send_date[strcspn(new_package->send_date, "\n")] = '\0';

  int option;
  printf("Enter package type (1: Basic, 2: Advanced, 3: Overnight): ");
  scanf("%d", &option);
  getchar();

  switch (option)
  {
  case 1:
    new_package->package_type = Basic;
    break;
  case 2:
    new_package->package_type = Advanced;
    break;
  case 3:
    new_package->package_type = Overnight;
    break;
  default:
    printf("Error package type! Exiting...");
    exit(1);
  }

  new_package->cost = calculate_cost(new_package);

  new_package->next = head;
  head = new_package;

  save_packages();
  printf("Package added successfully.\n");
}
```

Listing 4-5 package.c

After the user has entered all the package details, we calculate the package cost, and we insert the package in the front of the linked list. Then we proceed with saving the package list into the text file.

Next, we have the package deletion function:

```c
// remove a package from the linked list
void remove_package()
{
  char search_address[100];
  printf("Enter sender or delivery address of the package to remove: ");
  fgets(search_address, sizeof(search_address), stdin);
  search_address[strcspn(search_address, "\n")] = '\0';

  Package* current = head;
  Package* prev = NULL;

  while (current != NULL)
  {
    // Check if the sender or delivery address matches the search address
    if (strcmp(current->sender_address, search_address) == 0 ||
      strcmp(current->delivery_address, search_address) == 0)
    {
      if (prev == NULL)
      {
        // removing the head of the list
        head = current->next;
      }
      else
      {
        prev->next = current->next;
      }
      free(current);
      save_packages();
      printf("Package removed successfully.\n");
      return;
    }
    prev = current;
    current = current->next;
  }

  printf("Package with address '%s' not found.\n", search_address);
}
```


Here, we try to match the package sender or destination address. If found, the package is removed from the linked list, and the list is again saved into the text file.

Finally, we provide the function to list all the existing packages:

```c
// view all packages in the linked list
void view_packages()
{
```

```c
  Package* current = head;
  char* package_types_str[3] = { "Basic", "Advanced", "Overnight" };

  printf("List of Packages:\n");
  printf("Sender Address | Delivery Address | Weight | Send Date | Package Type |
Cost\n");
  while (current != NULL)
  {
    printf("%14s | %16s | %6.2f | %9s | %12s | %4.2f\n", current->sender_address,
      current->delivery_address, current->weight, current->send_date,
      package_types_str[current->package_type], current->cost);
    current = current->next;
  }
}
```

Listing 4-7: package.c

You can find this project in GitHub:

https://github.com/htset/advanced_c_exercises/tree/master/Packages

5. University Courses

Let's create a program that will handle the enrollment for courses at a university. Each course has one or more prerequisites, i.e. courses that must have been completed by a student in order to be able to enroll in the specific one.

Proposed Solution

First of all, we will define the structure for a university course:

```c
#include <stdio.h>
#include <stdbool.h>
#include <string.h>

#define MAX_COURSES 100

// Structure to represent a course
typedef struct
{
    int id;
    char name[50];
    int prereqCount;
    int prereqIDs[MAX_COURSES]; // IDs of prerequisite courses
} Course;
```


Each course contains an array of the IDs of the prerequisite courses.

We also have a structure about the student and the courses that have been completed successfully:

```c
// Structure to represent a student
typedef struct
{
    int id;
    char name[50];
    int courses[MAX_COURSES];
    int courseCount;
} Student;
```


Next, we define the function that finds out whether a student can enroll at a course:

```c
// Check if a student can enroll in a course
bool canEnroll(Student student, Course course)
{
    for (int i = 0; i < course.prereqCount; ++i)
    {
        bool hasPrereq = false;
        for (int j = 0; j < student.courseCount; ++j)
        {
            if (student.courses[j] == course.prereqIDs[i])
```

```c
    {
      hasPrereq = true;
      break;
    }
  }
  if (!hasPrereq)
  {
    return false;
  }
}
return true;
}
```


For each prerequisite course, this function tries to match it with a course already taken by the student.

Finally, the `main()` function:

```c
int main()
{
  // Sample course data
  Course courses[] = {
      {0, "Intro to Programming", 0},
      {1, "Data Structures", 1, {0}},
      {2, "Algorithms", 1, {1}},
      {3, "Database Management", 1, {0}},
      {4, "Web Development", 1, {0}},
      {5, "Operating Systems", 2, {1, 2}},
      {6, "Computer Networks", 2, {1, 5}},
      {7, "Software Engineering", 2, {1, 2}},
      {8, "Machine Learning", 2, {1, 2}},
      {9, "Distributed Systems", 1, {5}},
      {10, "Cybersecurity", 2, {2, 3}},
      {11, "Cloud Computing", 2, {2, 3}},
      {12, "Mobile App Development", 1, {4}},
      {13, "Game Development", 1, {0}},
      {14, "Artificial Intelligence", 2, {2, 8}},
      {15, "Big Data Analytics", 2, {2, 3}},
      {16, "Blockchain Technology", 2, {2, 3}},
      {17, "UI/UX Design", 1, {14}},
      {18, "Embedded Systems", 2, {1, 5}},
      {19, "Computer Graphics", 1, {0}}
  };

  courses[0].prereqIDs[0] = -1; // Assuming -1 represents no prerequisite

  // Create a sample student
  Student student;
  student.id = 1;
  strcpy(student.name, "John Doe");
  student.courseCount = 5;
  student.courses[0] = 0; // Intro to Programming
```

```c
    student.courses[1] = 1; // Data Structures
    student.courses[2] = 2; // Algorithms
    student.courses[3] = 3; // Database Management
    student.courses[4] = 4; // Web Development

    // Check if the student can enroll in specific courses
    Course targetCourses[] = {
        courses[13], // Game Development
        courses[16], // Blockchain Technology
        courses[17], // UI/UX Design (student cannot enroll)
        courses[18]  // Embedded Systems
    };

    printf("Enrollment status for %s:\n", student.name);
    for (int i = 0; i < 4; ++i)
    { // Loop through all four courses
      if (canEnroll(student, targetCourses[i]))
      {
        printf("- Can enroll in %s.\n", targetCourses[i].name);
      }
      else
      {
        printf("- Cannot enroll in %s due to missing prerequisites.\n",
targetCourses[i].name);
      }
    }

    return 0;
}
```

Listing 5-4: universityCourses.c

We create sample courses and a sample user that is still at the earlier stages of studies. We then try to find out if this student can enroll at 4 specific courses. We will see that the student will not be able to enroll at the most advanced ones, for lack of passed prerequisite courses.

You can find this project in GitHub:

https://github.com/htset/advanced_c_exercises/tree/master/UniversityCourses

6. Library

We will create a console application for a library. Users will be able to enter books and list all the title available in the library. They will also be able to lend books, return books as well as list all the book lending events. The books and and the lending events will be stored in binary files.

Proposed Solution

Let's begin with the definition of the `Book` and `LendingEvent` structs:

```c
#include <stdio.h>
#include <stdlib.h>
#include <string.h>
#include <time.h>

typedef struct
{
  char title[100];
  char author[100];
  int available;
} Book;

typedef struct
{
  char bookTitle[100];
  char userName[100];
  time_t lendingDate;
  int returned;
} LendingEvent;
```

Listing 6-1: library.c

For each book, we record the title and the author. We also keep information about whether is available or is currently lent.

For each lending event we record the book title and the name of the library user that has borrowed it. We also keep the lending date as well as a boolean value of whether it has been returned or not.

Next, we implement the functionality to add a new book in library catalog:

```c
void book_add(FILE* file)
{
  Book book;
  printf("Book title: ");
  fgets(book.title, sizeof(book.title), stdin);
  // Check if the user input was longer that the array size
  if (strlen(book.title) >= sizeof(book.title) - 1
      && book.title[sizeof(book.title) - 2] != '\n')
  {
    int c;
```

```c
    while ((c = getchar()) != '\n' && c != EOF); // Discard excess characters
    printf("Book title is too long and has been truncated.\n");
}
else
{
    // Remove trailing newline
    book.title[strcspn(book.title, "\n")] = '\0';
}

printf("Author: ");
fgets(book.author, sizeof(book.author), stdin);
if (strlen(book.author) >= sizeof(book.author) - 1
    && book.author[sizeof(book.author) - 2] != '\n')
{
    int c;
    while ((c = getchar()) != '\n' && c != EOF);
    printf("Book author is too long and has been truncated.\n");
}
else
{
    book.author[strcspn(book.author, "\n")] = '\0';
}

book.available = 1;

// Seek to the end of the file
fseek(file, 0, SEEK_END);
// Add the book entry
fwrite(&book, sizeof(Book), 1, file);
printf("Book added successfully.\n");
}
```


The code here is a bit complicated, since we want to make sure that the user cannot enter a book title or author that is longer than the string capacity, to avoid situations like a buffer overflow. For this reason, when we use `fgets()`, we specify the maximum number of characters that will be read from the standard input:

```c
fgets(book.title, sizeof(book.title), stdin);
```

If the user enters a longer string, then we should ignore the excess characters, or else they will be used during the next `fgets()` invocation, at the point where we get the book author from the user.

```c
if (strlen(book.title) >= sizeof(book.title) - 1
    && book.title[sizeof(book.title) - 2] != '\n')
{
    int c;
    while ((c = getchar()) != '\n' && c != EOF); // Discard excess characters
    printf("Book title is too long and has been truncated.\n");
}
```

Function `fgets()` also removes the newline character from the input stream and adds it at the end of the string variable. We have to remove it from there by adding a '\0' character:

```c
else
{
    // Remove trailing newline
    book.title[strcspn(book.title, "\n")] = '\0';
}
```

Note the use of the `strcspn()` function in the code above. This function scans the first argument for the first occurrence of any of the characters that are part of second argument. Then it returns the number of characters of the first argument that were read before this first occurrence (the search includes the terminating null-characters). In this way we can change the newline character with the string terminating one.

After we get the book author from the user, we proceed with moving to the end of the file and writing the new book object at this point:

```c
// Seek to the end of the file
fseek(file, 0, SEEK_END);
// Add the book entry
fwrite(&book, sizeof(Book), 1, file);
```

Function `fseek()` moves the file cursor at a distance of zero bytes from the end (`SEEK_END`) of the file. We use the `fwrite()` function to write the whole object into the binary file; note that we pass the *address* of this object. The third argument means that we want to write one object from the &book array (book is viewed as an array by `fwrite()`, since we have passed its pointer as an argument).

Next, we implement the listing of the books:

```c
void book_list(FILE* file)
{
    fseek(file, 0, SEEK_SET);
    Book book;
    printf("Books available in the library:\n");
    while (fread(&book, sizeof(Book), 1, file) == 1)
    {
        printf("Title: %s\nAuthor: %s\n", book.title, book.author);
        printf("Available: %s\n", (book.available == 1) ? "True" : "False");
        printf("--------------------------------\n");
    }
}
```

Listing 6-3: library.c

Here, we move the file cursor to the beginning of the file (at an offset of zero from SEEK_SET) and we use fread() to read each book object from the binary file.

We proceed with the book lending functionality:

```c
void book_lend(FILE* booksFile, FILE* lendingFile)
{
  char bookTitle[100];
  char userName[100];
  printf("Enter the title of the book to lend: ");
  fgets(bookTitle, sizeof(bookTitle), stdin);
  if (strlen(bookTitle) >= sizeof(bookTitle) - 1
      && bookTitle[sizeof(bookTitle) - 2] != '\n')
  {
    int c;
    while ((c = getchar()) != '\n' && c != EOF);
    printf("Book title is too long and has been truncated.\n");
  }
  else
  {
    bookTitle[strcspn(bookTitle, "\n")] = '\0';
  }

  fseek(booksFile, 0, SEEK_SET);

  Book book;
  int bookFound = 0;
  while (fread(&book, sizeof(Book), 1, booksFile) == 1)
  {
    if (strcmp(book.title, bookTitle) == 0 && book.available)
    {
      book.available = 0;
      fseek(booksFile, -((long)sizeof(Book)), SEEK_CUR);
      fwrite(&book, sizeof(Book), 1, booksFile);
      bookFound = 1;

      printf("Enter your name: ");
      fgets(userName, sizeof(userName), stdin);
      userName[strcspn(userName, "\n")] = '\0';
      if (strlen(userName) >= sizeof(userName) - 1
          && userName[sizeof(userName) - 2] != '\n')
      {
        int c;
        while ((c = getchar()) != '\n' && c != EOF);
        printf("User name is too long and has been truncated.\n");
      }
      else
      {
        userName[strcspn(userName, "\n")] = '\0';
      }

      // Record lending event
      LendingEvent event;
      strcpy(event.bookTitle, bookTitle);
```

```c
        strcpy(event.userName, userName);
        event.lendingDate = time(NULL);
        event.returned = 0;

        fseek(lendingFile, 0, SEEK_END);
        fwrite(&event, sizeof(LendingEvent), 1, lendingFile);
        printf("Book '%s' has been lent to %s.\n", bookTitle, userName);
        break;
      }
    }
  if (!bookFound)
  {
    printf("Book '%s' not found or not available.\n", bookTitle);
  }
}
```


We first try to find the requested book by reading through the books file. When we find the book (and if it is available), we mark it as not available and we write the book back to the file. To perform this, we move the file cursor back by `sizeof(Book)` bytes (that's why we use a negative offset value):

```c
fseek(booksFile, -((long)sizeof(Book)), SEEK_CUR);
```

In this way, we go back to the beginning of the specific entry in the file, and we overwrite it:

```c
fwrite(&book, sizeof(Book), 1, booksFile);
```

Afterwards, we record the lending event by writing a new entry at the end of the respective binary file.

Next, we present the functionality for returning a book:

```c
void book_return(FILE* booksFile, FILE* lendingFile)
{
  char bookTitle[100];
  printf("Enter the title of the book to return: ");
  fgets(bookTitle, sizeof(bookTitle), stdin);
  if (strlen(bookTitle) >= sizeof(bookTitle) - 1
    && bookTitle[sizeof(bookTitle) - 2] != '\n')
  {
    int c;
    while ((c = getchar()) != '\n' && c != EOF);
    printf("Book title is too long and has been truncated.\n");
  }
  else
  {
    bookTitle[strcspn(bookTitle, "\n")] = '\0';
  }
```

```c
    fseek(booksFile, 0, SEEK_SET);

    Book book;
    int bookFound = 0;
    while (fread(&book, sizeof(Book), 1, booksFile) == 1)
    {
      if (strcmp(book.title, bookTitle) == 0 && !book.available)
      {
        book.available = 1;
        fseek(booksFile, -((long)sizeof(Book)), SEEK_CUR);
        fwrite(&book, sizeof(Book), 1, booksFile);
        bookFound = 1;

        // Update lending record
        fseek(lendingFile, 0, SEEK_SET);
        LendingEvent event;
        while (fread(&event, sizeof(LendingEvent), 1, lendingFile) == 1)
        {
          if (strcmp(event.bookTitle, bookTitle) == 0 && !event.returned)
          {
            event.returned = 1;
            fseek(lendingFile, -((long)sizeof(LendingEvent)), SEEK_CUR);
            fwrite(&event, sizeof(LendingEvent), 1, lendingFile);
            printf("Book '%s' has been returned.\n", bookTitle);
            break;
          }
        }
        break;
      }
    }
    if (!bookFound)
    {
      printf("Book '%s' not found or already returned.\n", bookTitle);
    }
}
```


Here, we search in the lending events file for an event about the specific book and we modify the entry by setting the returned variable to 1.

Now, let's see the events listing function:

```c
void lending_events_list(FILE* lendingFile)
{
  fseek(lendingFile, 0, SEEK_SET);
  LendingEvent event;
  printf("Lending events:\n");
  while (fread(&event, sizeof(LendingEvent), 1, lendingFile) == 1)
  {
    printf("Book Title: %s\n", event.bookTitle);
    printf("User Name: %s\n", event.userName);
    printf("Lending Date: %s", ctime(&event.lendingDate));
    printf("Returned: %s\n", (event.returned == 1)? "True": "False");
    printf("----------------------------\n");
```

```c
    printf("\n");
  }
}
```

Listing 6-6: library.c

And finally, the `main()` function:

```c
int main()
{
  FILE* booksFile = fopen("books.bin", "rb+");
  if (booksFile == NULL)
  {
    booksFile = fopen("books.bin", "wb+");
    if (booksFile == NULL)
    {
      printf("Error opening books file.\n");
      return 1;
    }
  }

  FILE* lendingFile = fopen("lending_events.bin", "rb+");
  if (lendingFile == NULL)
  {
    lendingFile = fopen("lending_events.bin", "wb+");
    if (lendingFile == NULL)
    {
      printf("Error opening lending events file.\n");
      return 1;
    }
  }

  int choice;
  do
  {
    printf("\n1. Add a book\n2. List all books\n3. Lend a book\n4. Return a book\n5. List lending events\n0. Exit\n");
    printf("Enter your choice: ");
    scanf("%d", &choice);
    getchar(); // Consume newline left in the buffer by scanf

    switch (choice)
    {
    case 1:
      book_add(booksFile);
      break;
    case 2:
      book_list(booksFile);
      break;
    case 3:
      book_lend(booksFile, lendingFile);
      break;
    case 4:
      book_return(booksFile, lendingFile);
      break;
```

```c
    case 5:
      lending_events_list(lendingFile);
      break;
    case 0:
      printf("Exiting.\n");
      break;
    default:
      printf("Invalid choice. Please try again.\n");
    }
  } while (choice != 0);

  fclose(booksFile);
  fclose(lendingFile);
  return 0;
}
```


Here, we open the files as binary. If the files do not already exist, we will have to create them:

```c
FILE* booksFile = fopen("books.bin", "rb+");
if (booksFile == NULL)
{
  booksFile = fopen("books.bin", "wb+");
  if (booksFile == NULL)
  {
    printf("Error opening books file.\n");
    return 1;
  }
}
```

The main loop handles the interaction with the user. At the end, we should not forget to close both files.

You can find this project in GitHub:

https://github.com/htset/advanced_c_exercises/tree/master/Library

7. Contact List

In this exercise, we will create a list that will store the names and the phone numbers of our contacts. For faster search performance, the contacts will be stored in a *hash map* structure.

Proposed Solution

A *hash map*, also known as a *hash table*, is a data structure that efficiently organizes and retrieves data based on key-value pairs. It employs a technique called *hashing*, where each key is mapped to a unique index in an array using a hash function. This mapping allows for rapid insertion, deletion, and retrieval of values based on their associated keys.

In cases where multiple keys hash to the same index (known as *collisions*), hash maps often employ strategies such as *chaining* to handle these collisions gracefully and maintain performance.

Here is the definition of the structs used:

```c
#include <stdio.h>
#include <stdlib.h>
#include <string.h>

#define HASH_SIZE 100

typedef struct Contact
{
    char name[50];
    char phone[20];
    struct Contact* next;
} Contact;

typedef struct HashMap
{
    Contact* bucket_table[HASH_SIZE];
} HashMap;
```

Listing 7-1: contacts.c

The `HashMap` structure contains a table of 100 entries. Each entry contains a pointer to a `Contact` object. The `Contact` struct contains the name and the phone number, as well as a pointer to another Contact object, making it a linked list. Essentially, the `HashMap` struct is an array of linked lists; in this way the contact list can expand as we add new elements, avoiding collisions.

A contact will be instered into one of the buckets according to its specific hash number. We will use a hash function that will create a number between 0 and 99 based on the contact's name string:

```c
unsigned int hash(const char* name)
{
    unsigned int hash = 0;
```

```c
  int c;
  while (c = *name++)
  {
    hash = ((hash << 5) + hash) + c;
  }
  return hash % HASH_SIZE;
}
```


This function is based on a hash function written by Daniel J. Bernstein (also know as *djb*)[1]. This function returns the index of the hash map, where we should insert the specific contact.

First of all, we should initialize the HashMap struct by placing NULLs in the buckets:

```c
void contact_init(HashMap* phonebook)
{
  for (int i = 0; i < HASH_SIZE; i++)
  {
    phonebook->bucket_table[i] = NULL;
  }
}
```


Here is the code for the contact addition:

```c
void contact_add(HashMap* phonebook, const char* name, const char* phone)
{
  unsigned int hash_index = hash(name);
  Contact* new_contact = (Contact*)malloc(sizeof(Contact));
  if (!new_contact)
  {
    printf("Memory allocation failed.\n");
    return;
  }
  strcpy(new_contact->name, name);
  strcpy(new_contact->phone, phone);
  new_contact->next = phonebook->bucket_table[hash_index];
  phonebook->bucket_table[hash_index] = new_contact;
}
```


We first calculate the index based on the contact's name. Then we create a new Contact object. After populating the object variables, we insert the object at the beginning of the respective bucket.

Here is the code for contact removal:

```c
void contact_remove(HashMap* phonebook, const char* name)
```

----

[1] http://www.cse.yorku.ca/~oz/hash.html

```c
{
  unsigned int index = hash(name);
  Contact* contact = phonebook->bucket_table[index];
  Contact* previous = NULL;

  while (contact != NULL)
  {
    if (strcmp(contact->name, name) == 0)
    {
      if (previous == NULL)
      {
        // Contact to remove is the head of the list
        phonebook->bucket_table[index] = contact->next;
      }
      else
      {
        // Contact to remove is not the head of the list
        previous->next = contact->next;
      }
      free(contact);
      printf("Contact '%s' removed successfully.\n", name);
      return;
    }
    previous = contact;
    contact = contact->next;
  }
  printf("Contact '%s' not found.\n", name);
}
```


To remove an entry, we first need to get its hash value. We use this integer as index to get the respective bucket. We then search the bucket entries, one by one, until we locate the specific contact. We then remove the entry from the buckets, in the same way we remove a node from a linked list.

Next, the code for contact search is presented:

```c
void contact_search(HashMap* phonebook, const char* name)
{
  unsigned int hash_index = hash(name);
  Contact* contact = phonebook->bucket_table[hash_index];
  while (contact != NULL)
  {
    if (strcmp(contact->name, name) == 0)
    {
      printf("Name: %s\nPhone Number: %s\n", contact->name, contact->phone);
      return;
    }
    contact = contact->next;
  }
  printf("Contact '%s' not found.\n", name);
}
```

Finally, in the `main()` function, we create a phonebook and we use it to add, remove and search contacts:

```c
int main()
{
  HashMap phonebook;
  contact_init(&phonebook);

  contact_add(&phonebook, "John", "235454545");
  contact_add(&phonebook, "Jane", "775755454");
  contact_add(&phonebook, "George", "4344343477");

  contact_search(&phonebook, "John");
  contact_search(&phonebook, "Alex");
  contact_search(&phonebook, "George");

  contact_remove(&phonebook, "Jake");
  contact_remove(&phonebook, "Jane");
  contact_search(&phonebook, "Jane");

  return 0;
}
```


You can find this project in GitHub:

https://github.com/htset/advanced_c_exercises/tree/master/Contacts

8. Priority Todo List

We are going to implement a simple todo list application. Each entry will contain the task description as well as a number that will signify its priority (top priority is equal to 1).

The todo list will be implemented using a *linked list*. Apart from the options to add, delete and display tasks, there will also be functionality to sort the linked list using *bubble sort*.

Proposed Solution

Let's start with the definition of the linked list structure:

```c
#include <stdio.h>
#include <stdlib.h>
#include <string.h>

typedef struct Task
{
  char description[100];
  int priority;
  struct Task* next;
} Task;

typedef struct LinkedList
{
  Task* head;
  int size;
} LinkedList;
```

Listing 8-1: todo.c

The linked list consists of `Task` nodes that get linked one to the other via the `next` pointer. Variable `head` points to the first element in the list.

First let's see the `main()` function:

```c
void init_tasks(LinkedList* list);
void add_task(LinkedList* list, const char* description, int priority);
void remove_task(LinkedList* list, int index);
void display_tasks(LinkedList* list);
void sort_tasks(LinkedList* list);

int main()
{
  LinkedList list;
  init_tasks(&list);

  int choice;
  char description[100];
  int priority;
  int index;

  do
```

```c
{
    printf("\nTo-Do List Manager\n");
    printf("1. Add Task\n");
    printf("2. Remove Task\n");
    printf("3. Display Tasks\n");
    printf("4. Sort Tasks by Priority\n");
    printf("0. Exit\n");
    printf("Enter your choice: ");
    scanf("%d", &choice);

    switch (choice)
    {
    case 1:
      printf("Enter task description: ");
      getchar(); // Clear input buffer
      fgets(description, sizeof(description), stdin);
      description[strcspn(description, "\n")] = '\0'; // Remove trailing newline
      printf("Enter priority: ");
      scanf("%d", &priority);
      add_task(&list, description, priority);
      printf("Task added successfully.\n");
      break;
    case 2:
      printf("Enter number of task to remove: ");
      scanf("%d", &index);
      remove_task(&list, index-1);
      printf("Task removed successfully.\n");
      break;
    case 3:
      printf("List of tasks:\n");
      display_tasks(&list);
      break;
    case 4:
      sort_tasks(&list);
      printf("Tasks sorted by priority.\n");
      break;
    case 5:
      printf("Exiting...\n");
      break;
    default:
      printf("Invalid choice. Please try again.\n");
    }
  } while (choice != 0);

  return 0;
}
```

Listing 8-2: todo.c

The init_tasks() function initializes the linked list structure:

```c
void init_tasks(LinkedList* list)
{
  list->head = NULL;
  list->size = 0;
```

```
}
```


The add_task() function allocates memory for a new task node and inserts it at the end of the list:

```c
void add_task(LinkedList* list, const char* description, int priority)
{
  Task* task = (Task*)malloc(sizeof(Task));
  if (!task)
  {
    printf("Memory allocation failed.\n");
    return;
  }
  strcpy(task->description, description);
  task->priority = priority;
  task->next = NULL;

  if (list->head == NULL)
  {
    // List is empty
    list->head = task;
  }
  else
  {
    Task* temp = list->head;
    // Find the last node
    while (temp->next != NULL)
    {
      temp = temp->next;
    }
    // Insert the new task after the last node
    temp->next = task;
  }
  list->size++;
}
```


Next, we define the remove_task() function:

```c
void remove_task(LinkedList* list, int index)
{
  if (list->head == NULL)
  {
    printf("List is empty.\n");
    return;
  }

  if (index == 0)
  {
    // If we remove the first item in the list
    Task* temp = list->head;
```

```c
        list->head = list->head->next;
        free(temp);
        list->size--;
        return;
    }

    Task* previous = NULL;
    Task* current = list->head;
    int i = 0;
    // Go to the selected index
    while (current != NULL && i < index)
    {
        previous = current;
        current = current->next;
        i++;
    }

    if (current == NULL)
    {
        printf("Index out of bounds.\n");
        return;
    }

    previous->next = current->next;
    free(current);
    list->size--;
}
```


The second argument to the function is the index of the entry inside the linked list, as it is presented during listing. As we will see in the next snippet, we start listing the tasks from number 1, which is something that we take into account in the calculations above.

Here is the code for the task listing:

```c
void display_tasks(LinkedList* list)
{
    Task* temp = list->head;
    int i = 1;
    while (temp != NULL)
    {
        printf("%d) Description: %s, Priority: %d\n",
            i++, temp->description, temp->priority);
        temp = temp->next;
    }
}
```


Finally, we present the code for the sorting of tasks according to their priority:

```c
void sort_tasks(LinkedList* list)
{
```

```c
  int swapped;
  Task* ptr1;
  Task* ptr2 = NULL;

  if (list->head == NULL)
    return;

  do
  {
    swapped = 0; // will change if swapping happens
    ptr1 = list->head;

    while (ptr1->next != ptr2)
    {
      if (ptr1->priority > ptr1->next->priority)
      {
        // Swap data of adjacent nodes
        int tempPriority = ptr1->priority;
        ptr1->priority = ptr1->next->priority;
        ptr1->next->priority = tempPriority;

        char tempDescription[100];
        strcpy(tempDescription, ptr1->description);
        strcpy(ptr1->description, ptr1->next->description);
        strcpy(ptr1->next->description, tempDescription);

        swapped = 1; // swap happened in this loop pass; don't stop yet
      }
      ptr1 = ptr1->next;
    }
    ptr2 = ptr1;
  } while (swapped); // quit loop when no swap happened
}
```


The code employs the *bubble sort* algorithm to perform the tasks sorting operation. In bubble sort, we perform multiple passes of the linked list. Each time we find a task that has lower priority than its next task, then we perform swapping of those adjacent tasks. Over time, all entries will be sorted according to priority and there will eventually be a loop pass where no swapping will occur. This is when the algorithm will end.

You can find this project in GitHub:

https://github.com/htset/advanced_c_exercises/tree/master/Todo

9. Songs List

Let's create a simple program that takes an array of songs and sorts them by artist, album or release date, using *insertion sort*.

Proposed Solution

The Song structure will contain information about the title of the song, the artist, the album and the release year:

```c
#include <stdio.h>
#include <stdlib.h>
#include <string.h>

typedef struct
{
    char title[100];
    char artist[100];
    char album[100];
    int release_year;
} Song;
```

Listing 9-1: songs.c

Next, we define three functions, that will be used for the comparisons:

```c
// Compare songs based on artist
int compareByArtist(const Song* a, const Song* b)
{
    return strcmp(a->artist, b->artist);
}

// Compare songs based on album
int compareByAlbum(const Song* a, const Song* b)
{
    return strcmp(a->album, b->album);
}

// Compare songs based on release date
int compareByReleaseDate(const Song* a, const Song* b)
{
    return (a->release_year - b->release_year);
}
```

Listing 9-2: songs.c

In the first two functions, we compare two strings, while in the third one we compare two integers. Those functions will be used by the `insertionSort()` function:

```c
void insertionSort(Song arr[], int n, int (*compare)(const Song*, const Song*))
{
    int i, j;
    Song key;
    for (i = 1; i < n; i++)
```

```c
{
    key = arr[i];
    j = i - 1;

    // Move elements of arr[0..i-1], that are greater than key,
    // to one position ahead of their current position
    while (j >= 0 && compare(&arr[j], &key) > 0)
    {
        arr[j + 1] = arr[j];
        j = j - 1;
    }
    arr[j + 1] = key;
    }
}
```

Listing 9-3: songs.c

First of all, we should note that we pass a function pointer (compare) as argument to insertionSort(). Function pointers in C contain the address of a function and can be used to create a callback mechanism. More specifically, when insertSort() calls compare(), it essentially calls the function whose pointer was passed when insertSort() was called.

For instance, if we call insertionSort() like this:

```c
insertionSort(songs, num_songs, compareByArtist);
```

then, the following code inside insertionSort():

```c
while (j >= 0 && compare(&arr[j], &key) > 0)
```

will result in calling the compareByArtist() function. In this way, we don't have to write insertionSort() three times to accommodate for the three different types of comparison.

Insertion sort works by taking each element in the array and moving it to the left part of the array in a sorted position. At any time, the left part of the array is sorted, while we take items from the right part. As we move an element to a place in the array, all the items to the right will have to move one place to the right.

This is all illustrated in the main() function where we call insertionSort() three times, each time passing a different comparison function. Each time, the array is sorted in a different way:

```c
int main()
{
    Song songs[] = {
        {"Song1", "Artist2", "Album1", 2010},
        {"Song2", "Artist1", "Album2", 2005},
        {"Song3", "Artist3", "Album1", 2015},
        {"Song4", "Artist4", "Album3", 2008},
        {"Song5", "Artist1", "Album2", 2003},
```

```c
      {"Song6", "Artist3", "Album4", 2019},
      {"Song7", "Artist2", "Album3", 2012},
      {"Song8", "Artist4", "Album4", 2017},
      {"Song9", "Artist5", "Album5", 2014},
      {"Song10", "Artist5", "Album5", 2011} };

  int num_songs = sizeof(songs) / sizeof(songs[0]);

  // Sort by artist
  insertionSort(songs, num_songs, compareByArtist);
  printf("Sorted by Artist:\n");
  for (int i = 0; i < num_songs; i++)
  {
    printf("%s by %s\n", songs[i].title, songs[i].artist);
  }
  printf("\n");

  // Sort by album
  insertionSort(songs, num_songs, compareByAlbum);
  printf("Sorted by Album:\n");
  for (int i = 0; i < num_songs; i++)
  {
    printf("%s from %s\n", songs[i].title, songs[i].album);
  }
  printf("\n");

  // Sort by release date
  insertionSort(songs, num_songs, compareByReleaseDate);
  printf("Sorted by Release Date:\n");
  for (int i = 0; i < num_songs; i++)
  {
    printf("%s released in %d\n", songs[i].title, songs[i].release_year);
  }

  return 0;
}
```

Listing 9-4: songs.c

You can find this project in GitHub:

https://github.com/htset/advanced_c_exercises/tree/master/Songs

10. Syntax Checker

We will create a trivial syntax checker that will scan a source code file and will determine whether the parentheses, brackets, or braces in the code are balanced or not.

Proposed Solution

In the source code, when we open a series of parentheses, brackets, or braces, we have to make sure that they are closed in the reverse order. The fact that items entered in a *stack* are extracted in the reverse order, makes it suitable for this algorithm.

Therefore, we will use a stack to track the opened parentheses, brackets, and braces:

```c
#include <stdio.h>
#include <stdlib.h>

#define MAX_SIZE 100

typedef struct
{
  char items[MAX_SIZE];
  int top;
} Stack;
```

Listing 10-1: syntaxChecker.c

Here is the code for the stack initialization:

```c
void stack_init(Stack* s)
{
  s->top = -1;
}
```

Listing 10-2: syntaxChecker.c

Next, we add the code for stack *push* and *pop*, as well as a function to check if the stack is empty:

```c
void stack_push(Stack* s, char c)
{
  if (s->top == MAX_SIZE - 1)
  {
    printf("Stack is full\n");
    exit(1);
  }
  s->items[++s->top] = c;
}

char stack_pop(Stack* s)
{
  if (s->top == -1)
  {
    printf("Stack is empty\n");
```

```c
    exit(1);
  }
  return s->items[s->top--];
}

int stack_check_empty(Stack* s)
{
  return s->top == -1;
}
```


The interesting part of the code is the algorithm that checks whether the file is balanced:

```c
int check_balanced(char* filename)
{
  FILE* file = fopen(filename, "r");
  if (file == NULL)
  {
    printf("Error opening file.\n");
    exit(1);
  }

  char c;
  Stack stack;
  stack_init(&stack);

  while ((c = fgetc(file)) != EOF)
  {
    if (c == '(' || c == '[' || c == '{')
    {
      stack_push(&stack, c);
    }
    else if (c == ')' || c == ']' || c == '}')
    {
      // If stack is empty --> Return 'Unbalanced'
      if (stack_check_empty(&stack))
      {
        fclose(file);
        return 0;
      }
      char openingChar = stack_pop(&stack);
      if ((c == ')' && openingChar != '(') ||
          (c == ']' && openingChar != '[') ||
          (c == '}' && openingChar != '{'))
      {
        fclose(file);
        // If closing character doesn't match top of stack
        // --> return 'Unbalanced'
        return 0;
      }
    }
  }

  // If stack is empty, after we have finished
```

```c
    // checking the input file
    // --> return 'Balanced'
    int result = stack_check_empty(&stack);
    fclose(file);
    return result;
}
```


We open and parse that source code file, and we push the bracket opening characters into the stack. When we encounter a closing character, then we pop the first available opening character from the stack.

If there is a mismatch between those two characters, we conclude that the file is not balanced. At the end, we also check that the stack is emptied; if not, then the file is still unbalanced.

Note that this is a trivial version of the algorithm. In fact, if we try to check the exercises's own source file for parentheses balancing, we will get an error – even though the code compiles. That's because we use single characters (opening or closing) in our code during checking, like in the following line:

```c
if (c == '(' || c == '[' || c == '{')
```

A more advanced version of the algorithm would not take those characters (e.g. those enclosed in quotes) into account.

You can find this project in GitHub:

https://github.com/htset/advanced_c_exercises/tree/master/SyntaxChecker

11. Maze Solver

In this exercise, we will use a *stack* to find our way through a maze.

Proposed Solution

We will define a maze as a two-dimensional array of integers. The walls will be marked with ones (1), while the corridors of the maze will be marked with zeroes (0).

Below, we can see the definition of a 15x15 maze:

```c
#include <stdio.h>
#include <stdlib.h>

#define ROWS 15
#define COLS 15

int maze[ROWS][COLS] = {
    {0, 1, 0, 0, 0, 0, 0, 0, 0, 0, 0, 0, 0, 0, 0},
    {0, 1, 0, 1, 0, 1, 1, 1, 1, 0, 1, 1, 1, 1, 0},
    {0, 1, 0, 1, 0, 1, 0, 0, 0, 0, 1, 0, 0, 0, 0},
    {0, 0, 0, 1, 0, 1, 0, 1, 1, 1, 1, 0, 1, 1, 0},
    {0, 1, 0, 1, 0, 1, 0, 0, 0, 0, 1, 0, 1, 0, 0},
    {0, 1, 0, 1, 0, 1, 1, 1, 1, 0, 1, 0, 1, 1, 0},
    {0, 1, 0, 1, 0, 0, 0, 0, 1, 0, 1, 0, 0, 0, 0},
    {0, 1, 0, 1, 1, 1, 1, 0, 1, 0, 1, 0, 1, 1, 0},
    {0, 1, 0, 0, 0, 0, 1, 0, 1, 0, 1, 0, 0, 1, 0},
    {0, 1, 1, 1, 1, 0, 1, 0, 1, 0, 1, 0, 1, 1, 0},
    {0, 0, 0, 0, 1, 0, 1, 0, 1, 0, 1, 0, 0, 0, 0},
    {0, 1, 1, 0, 1, 0, 1, 0, 1, 0, 1, 1, 1, 1, 0},
    {0, 0, 1, 0, 1, 0, 0, 0, 1, 0, 0, 0, 0, 1, 0},
    {0, 1, 1, 1, 1, 1, 1, 1, 1, 1, 1, 1, 0, 1, 0},
    {0, 0, 0, 0, 0, 0, 0, 0, 0, 0, 0, 0, 0, 1, 0}
};
```

Listing 11-1: mazeSolver.c

The entrance of the maze is at the top left corner, and the exit at the bottom right corner.

We will use a stack structure to solve this maze. As we move through the maze, we store the entered point coordinates in the stack. When we reach a dead end, then we will have to backtrack, and we will do this by popping one point from the stack. This algorithm is called *Depth-first search (DFS)*, as it goes inside the maze as deep as possible, only to go back and try another direction when no way is found.

Here is the code for the stack:

```c
struct Point
{
    int row, col;
};

struct Stack
```

```c
{
  struct Point* points;
  int top;
};

void stack_init(struct Stack* stack, int capacity)
{
  stack->points = (struct Point*)malloc(capacity * sizeof(struct Point));
  stack->top = -1;
}

int stack_is_empty(struct Stack* stack)
{
  return stack->top == -1;
}

void stack_push(struct Stack* stack, int x, int y)
{
  stack->top++;
  stack->points[stack->top].row = x;
  stack->points[stack->top].col = y;
}

struct Point stack_pop(struct Stack* stack)
{
  return stack->points[stack->top--];
}
```

Listing 11-2: mazeSolver.c

The stack contains an array of point coordinates. We have defined functions to initialize the stack, to check if it's empty, as well as to push and pop Point objects in the stack.

Next, we add the code to check whether we can move to a cell:

```c
// Check if we can move to this cell
int canMove(int row, int col)
{
  return (row >= 0 && row < ROWS && col >= 0 && col < COLS && maze[row][col] == 0);
}
```

Listing 11-3: mazeSolver.c

We also provide a function to print the maze:

```c
void printMaze(int maze[ROWS][COLS])
{
  for (int i = 0; i < ROWS; i++) {
    for (int j = 0; j < COLS; j++)
    {
      printf("%d ", maze[i][j]);
    }
    printf("\n");
  }
```

```
}
```


The following function implements the maze solving algorithm:

```c
// Solve the maze using backtracking
int solveMaze(struct Stack *stack, int row, int col)
{
  if (row == ROWS - 1 && col == COLS - 1)
  {
    // destination reached
    stack_push(stack, row, col);
    return 1;
  }

  if (canMove(row, col))
  {
    stack_push(stack, row, col);
    maze[row][col] = 2; // Marking visited

    // Move right
    if (solveMaze(stack, row, col + 1))
      return 1;

    // Move down
    if (solveMaze(stack, row + 1, col))
      return 1;

    // Move left
    if (solveMaze(stack, row, col - 1))
      return 1;

    // Move up
    if (solveMaze(stack, row - 1, col))
      return 1;

    // If none of the above movements work, backtrack
    stack_pop(stack);
    return 0;
  }

  return 0;
}
```


First of all, we check whether the destination has been reached, by comparing the current
row and column with the constant values ROW and COL.

In the opposite case, we first check if we can actually move to this cell, i.e if it is part of a
corridor and is within the maze bounds. If so, we add its coordinates into the stack and we
mark the cell with the number 2, to mark that we have passed from this cell.

Then, we proceed with calling recursively the `solveMaze()` function for all four directions, starting with right and down, and then trying with left and up. If none of those movements results in solving the maze (i.e. they all return 0), then we will have to backtrack. Since this point in the maze was not eventually part of the solution, we pop it from the stack.

Finally, let's see the main function of the program:

```c
int main()
{
  struct Stack stack;
  stack_init(&stack, ROWS*COLS);

  printf("This is the maze:\n");
  printMaze(maze);

  if (solveMaze(&stack, 0, 0))
  {
    printf("\n\n This is the path found:\n");
    while(!stack_is_empty(&stack)){
      struct Point p = stack_pop(&stack);
      printf("(%d, %d) ", p.row, p.col);
    }
    printf("\n\nThis is the maze with all the points crossed:\n");
    printMaze(maze);
  }
  else
  {
    printf("No path found\n");
  }
  return 0;
}
```

Listing 11-6: mazeSolver.c

We first print the initial maze, then we print the solution path, by popping the points from the stack, one-by-one. Then we display the map with all the points that we crossed marked with '2'.

You can find this project in GitHub:

https://github.com/htset/advanced_c_exercises/tree/master/MazeSolver

12. File Indexer

For this exercise, we will create a program that will recursively index all the files in a specified folder. The information about the indexed files (filename and location in the disk) will be stored in a *Binary Search Tree (BST)* for faster searching.

The Binary Search Tree structure is a tree where each node has only two children, left and right. Here is the definition of the structure:

```c
#include <stdio.h>
#include <stdlib.h>
#include <string.h>
#include <windows.h>

#ifdef _MSC_VER
#define strdup(p) _strdup(p)
#endif

typedef struct TreeNode
{
    char* filename;
    char* location;
    struct TreeNode* left;
    struct TreeNode* right;
}TreeNode;
```

Listing 12-1: fileIndexer.c

Each node of the tree contains two strings, the filename and the file location. It also contains pointers to the two children nodes.

Next, we define a function to allocate a new node:

```c
TreeNode* TreeNode_create(char* filename, char *location)
{
    TreeNode* node = (TreeNode*)malloc(sizeof(TreeNode));
    if(node == NULL)
    {
        printf("Memory allocation error. Exiting..\n");
        exit(1);
    }
    node->filename = strdup(filename);
    node->location = strdup(location);
    node->left = node->right = NULL;
    return node;
}
```

Listing 12-2: fileIndexer.c

Note the use of the `strdup()` function; it is used to duplicate a string. It gets as argument a string and returns a pointer to a new string that is a copy of the original. The Microsoft compiler version is _strdup(), that's why we make the #define at the top of the file. If the Microsoft compiler is detected (#ifdef _MSC_VER) then the #define is performed.

We insert a node into the tree with the Treenode_insert() function:

```c
TreeNode* TreeNode_insert(TreeNode* root, char* filename, char* location)
{
    // If the tree is empty, return a new node
    if (root == NULL)
      return TreeNode_create(filename, location);

    // If not empty, then go down the tree
    if (strcmp(filename, root->filename) < 0)
        root->left = TreeNode_insert(root->left, filename, location);
    else if (strcmp(filename, root->filename) > 0)
        root->right = TreeNode_insert(root->right, filename, location);

    // Return the root pointer, it is used
    // by the lines above
    return root;
}
```


We see that the Treenode_insert() function is *recursive*. Starting from the root of the tree, we move downwards to the left or to the right depending on the inserted value. The recursion ends when we hit the bottom of the tree (root == NULL). This is where the new entry is inserted.

Next, we define a function to recursively print the contents of the tree:

```c
void TreeNode_print(TreeNode* root)
{
    if (root != NULL)
    {
      TreeNode_print(root->left);
      printf("%s - (%s)\n", root->filename, root->location);
      TreeNode_print(root->right);
    }
}
```


The above defined functions are used by the index_file_system() function:

```c
void index_file_system(TreeNode** root, const char* path)
{
    WIN32_FIND_DATAA findData;
    HANDLE hFind;
    char searchPath[MAX_PATH];
    char subDirPath[MAX_PATH];

    // Create a search pattern --> get all files in the folder
```

```c
    snprintf(searchPath, MAX_PATH, "%s\\*", path);
    // Find the first file in the directory
    hFind = FindFirstFileA(searchPath, &findData);
    if (hFind == INVALID_HANDLE_VALUE)
    {
        printf("Error: Could not open directory.\n");
        return;
    }

    // Iterate over files in the directory
    do
    {
        if (!(findData.dwFileAttributes & FILE_ATTRIBUTE_DIRECTORY))
        {
            *root = TreeNode_insert(*root, findData.cFileName, path);
        }
        else if (strcmp(findData.cFileName, ".") != 0 && strcmp(findData.cFileName, "..")
!= 0)
        {
            snprintf(subDirPath, MAX_PATH, "%s\\%s", path, findData.cFileName);
            // Recursively index subdirectory
            index_file_system(root, subDirPath);
        }
    } while (FindNextFileA(hFind, &findData) != 0);

    // Close the search handle
    FindClose(hFind);
}
```


As we can see, it contains Windows specific code (hence the inclusion of the *windows.h* file at the top). We use functions `FindFirstFileA()` and `FindNextFileA()` to search in a folder, for files that follow a specific pattern.

Here, we use the asterisk (*) pattern, which means that all files in the specified folder should be returned by the search:

```c
    snprintf(searchPath, MAX_PATH, "%s\\*", path);
```

Function `FindFirstFileA()` opens a search handle and returns information about the first file that the file system finds with a name that matches the specified pattern. If the search fails (e.g. the folder name is not correct) then we get an invalid handle.

`FindFirstFileA()` returns a structure (`findData`) that contains information about the file (e.g. file name). It also tells us whether it is a folder or not. If it is a folder, then we will also recursively perform indexing on this too.

We use the returned handle and we call function `FindNextFileA()`in a loop, to get all the files in the folder, one by one. At the end of the indexing, we make sure to close the search and release the handle.

After the tree has been set up, we can call function `search_file_location()` to get the location of a file:

```c
// Search for a file in the BST
char* search_file_location(struct TreeNode* root, const char* filename)
{
  // Traverse the tree until a match is found or the tree is exhausted
  while (root != NULL)
  {
    int cmp = strcmp(filename, root->filename);
    if (cmp == 0)
    {
      return root->location; // File found
    }
    else if (cmp < 0)
    {
      root = root->left; // Search in the left subtree
    }
    else
    {
      root = root->right; // Search in the right subtree
    }
  }
  return NULL; // File not found
}
```

Listing 12-6: fileIndexer.c

We traverse the tree until we find a node with the specified file name. If the tree is exhausted, then we return NULL.

Finally, here is the `main()` function:

```c
int main(int argc, char* argv[])
{
  char path[200];
  printf("Path to index recursively: ");
  fgets(path, 200, stdin);
  path[strcspn(path, "\n")] = '\0';

  TreeNode* root = NULL;

  // Index the file system
  index_file_system(&root, path);

  // Print indexed files
  printf("Indexed Files:\n");
  TreeNode_print(root);
```

```c
  char filenameToSearch[200];
  printf("Let's search for a file's location. Give the file name: ");
  fgets(filenameToSearch, 200, stdin);
  filenameToSearch[strcspn(filenameToSearch, "\n")] = '\0';

  char* location = search_file_location(root, filenameToSearch);
  if (location != NULL)
  {
    printf("File '%s' found. Location: %s\n", filenameToSearch, location);
  }
  else
  {
    printf("File '%s' not found.\n", filenameToSearch);
  }
  return 0;
}
```


Users can index the contents of a folder and then they can search for a specific filename.

Proposed Solution (Linux)

In order to make this code work in Linux, then we have to change the implementation of index_file_system() like this:

```c
void index_file_system(struct TreeNode **root, const char *path)
{
  DIR *dir;
  struct dirent *entry;
  struct stat fileStat;

  // Open the directory
  dir = opendir(path);
  if (dir == NULL)
  {
    perror("opendir");
    return;
  }

  // Read directory entries
  while ((entry = readdir(dir)) != NULL)
  {
    if (strcmp(entry->d_name, ".") != 0 && strcmp(entry->d_name, "..") != 0)
    {
      char fullPath[PATH_MAX];
      snprintf(fullPath, PATH_MAX, "%s/%s", path, entry->d_name);

      // Check if it's a regular file
      if (stat(fullPath, &fileStat) == 0 && S_ISREG(fileStat.st_mode))
      {
        *root = TreeNode_insert(*root, entry->d_name, path);
```

```c
    }
    else if (S_ISDIR(fileStat.st_mode))
    {
      index_file_system(root, fullPath); // Recursively index subdirectory
    }
  }
}

  closedir(dir);
}
```


We will also have to add two #includes at the top:

```c
#include <dirent.h>
#include <sys/stat.h>
```

First, we open the directory specified by the user and then, we read all the entries that reside in it. After ignoring the current and previous directory entries (. and .. respectively), we check whether the entry is a simple file or a subdirectory. In the former case, we add it into the tree. In the latter case, we enter this directory, and we follow the same process recursively.

You can find this project in GitHub:

https://github.com/htset/advanced_c_exercises/tree/master/FileIndexer

https://github.com/htset/advanced_c_exercises/tree/master/FileIndexerLinux

13. Social Network

A social network is essentially a *graph* of nodes that depicts the users of the network along with their connections to their friends. In this exercise, we will create such a graph and we will implement the functionality to recommend new friends according to a user's current connections.

Proposed Solution

There are various ways to implement the users' graph, for example using *sparse two-dimensional matrices*. Here we will construct the graph with the use of a *one-dimensional array* of users, where the connections are stored in a linked list:

```c
#include <stdio.h>
#include <stdlib.h>
#include <string.h>

#define MAX_USERS 100
#define MAX_NAME_LENGTH 50

typedef struct Node
{
    char name[MAX_NAME_LENGTH];
    struct Node* next;
} Node;

typedef struct
{
    Node* head;
} LinkedList;

typedef struct
{
    char name[MAX_NAME_LENGTH];
    LinkedList friends;
} UserNode;

UserNode users[MAX_USERS];
int num_users = 0;
```


The `UserNode` struct contains the name of the user as well as a linked list of the user's friends. We also define as array of all the users of the social network.

Next, we define a *queue* structure that will be used by the friend recommendation algorithm:

```c
typedef struct QueueNode
{
    int user_index;
    struct QueueNode* next;
```

```c
} QueueNode;

typedef struct
{
  QueueNode* front;
  QueueNode* rear;
} Queue;

Queue* queue_create()
{
  Queue* queue = (Queue*)malloc(sizeof(Queue));
  queue->front = queue->rear = NULL;
  return queue;
}

int queue_is_empty(Queue* queue)
{
  return (queue->front == NULL);
}

void queue_enqueue(Queue* queue, int user_index)
{
  QueueNode* newNode = (QueueNode*)malloc(sizeof(QueueNode));
  newNode->user_index = user_index;
  newNode->next = NULL;

  if (queue_is_empty(queue))
  {
    queue->front = queue->rear = newNode;
  }
  else
  {
    queue->rear->next = newNode;
    queue->rear = newNode;
  }
}

int queue_dequeue(Queue* queue)
{
  if (queue_is_empty(queue))
  {
    printf("Queue is empty!\n");
    return -1;
  }

  QueueNode* temp = queue->front;
  int user_index = temp->user_index;
  queue->front = queue->front->next;

  if (queue->front == NULL)
  {
    queue->rear = NULL;
  }
```

```c
  free(temp);
  return user_index;
}
```


The queue contains the indexes of the users, as they appear inside the users' array. We define the queue nodes, the queue structs, as well as functions to enqueue and dequeue user indexes inside the queue. We also provide functions to create a queue and to check whether it is empty or not.

Now, let's see how we will insert users into the graph and how we will define the connections with their friends:

```c
void graph_add_user(char name[])
{
  if (num_users >= MAX_USERS)
  {
    printf("Max user limit reached!\n");
    return;
  }

  strcpy(users[num_users].name, name);
  users[num_users].friends.head = NULL;
  num_users++;
}

void graph_add_connection(int src, int dest)
{
  if (src < 0 || src >= num_users || dest < 0 || dest >= num_users)
  {
    printf("Invalid user index!\n");
    return;
  }

  Node* new_node_src = (Node*)malloc(sizeof(Node));
  strcpy(new_node_src->name, users[dest].name);
  new_node_src->next = users[src].friends.head;
  users[src].friends.head = new_node_src;

  Node* new_node_dest = (Node*)malloc(sizeof(Node));
  strcpy(new_node_dest->name, users[src].name);
  new_node_dest->next = users[dest].friends.head;
  users[dest].friends.head = new_node_dest;
}
```


Note that when we add a new connection, we make it bi-directional. That is, we insert a friend node for each one of the connection's ends.

Next, we proceed to the interesting stuff, the recommender function:

```c
void graph_recommend_friends(int user_index)
{
  printf("Recommended friends for %s:\n", users[user_index].name);

  Queue* queue = queue_create();
  int visited[MAX_USERS] = { 0 };

  visited[user_index] = 1;
  queue_enqueue(queue, user_index);

  while (!queue_is_empty(queue))
  {
    int current_user_index = queue_dequeue(queue);
    Node* current = users[current_user_index].friends.head;

    while (current != NULL)
    {
      int friend_index = -1;
      for (int i = 0; i < num_users; i++)
      {
        if (strcmp(current->name, users[i].name) == 0)
        {
          friend_index = i;
          break;
        }
      }

      if (friend_index != -1 && !visited[friend_index])
      {
        printf("- %s\n", current->name);
        visited[friend_index] = 1;
        queue_enqueue(queue, friend_index);
      }

      current = current->next;
    }
  }

  free(queue);
}
```


As already mentioned, the algorithm makes use of a queue. In the queue, we store the indexes of the user's friends as we follow the linked list. We then use the queue to get the friends of the user's friends, and in this way, we are able to travel through the connection of the graph and find all the connected people to the specific user.

Note that we are using the `visited[]` array to store the persons that we have already visited. This will prevent the algorithm for looping to the same friends again and again and will ensure the convergence of our search.

Finally, here is the `main()` function:

```c
int main()
{
  graph_add_user("User A");
  graph_add_user("User B");
  graph_add_user("User C");
  graph_add_user("User D");
  graph_add_user("User E");
  graph_add_user("User F");
  graph_add_user("User G");
  graph_add_user("User H");

  graph_add_connection(0, 1);
  graph_add_connection(1, 2);
  graph_add_connection(2, 3);
  graph_add_connection(4, 5);
  graph_add_connection(5, 7);
  graph_add_connection(3, 6);

  graph_recommend_friends(0);
  graph_recommend_friends(1);
  graph_recommend_friends(7);

  return 0;
}
```
Listing 13-5: socialNetwork.c

In main(), we add users to the graph and we enter their friend connections. Then we run the algorithm to get friend recommendations.

You can find this project in GitHub:

https://github.com/htset/advanced_c_exercises/tree/master/SocialNetwork

14. Inventory with AVL Tree

In this exercise, we will create an inventory program, that will store information about the comnpany's products in an AVL tree structure.

Proposed Solution

An *AVL (Adelson-Velsky and Landis) tree* is a *self-balancing* binary search tree structure. With the term *balanced*, we mean that both branches of the tree have the same depth or differ by one level at the most. To achieve this, a process called *rebalancing* is occasionally performed, that changes the tree structure in way that the tree is closer to be balanced.

The AVL tree has almost the same structure as a simple binary search tree (BST); the difference lies in the rebalancing algorithm. Let's see the structure:

```c
#include <stdio.h>
#include <stdlib.h>
#include <string.h>

typedef struct Product
{
    int id;
    char name[50];
    float price;
    int quantity;
} Product;

typedef struct InventoryNode
{
    Product product;
    struct InventoryNode* left;
    struct InventoryNode* right;
    int height;
} InventoryNode;
```

Listing 14-1: inventoryAVL.c

The `InventoryNode` struct contains a product object and two pointers to the tree's branches. Most importantly, it also contains the `height` property, which is used to track the tree's height.

Next, we define two functions for the AVL tree:

```c
int avl_get_height(InventoryNode* node)
{
    if (node == NULL)
        return 0;
    return node->height;
}

int avl_get_balance(InventoryNode* node)
{
```

```c
    if (node == NULL)
       return 0;
    return avl_get_height(node->left) - avl_get_height(node->right);
}
```


The former gives us the height of the tree, while the latter checks whether the tree is balanced or not.

Afterwards, we add code for the creation of a new node in the tree:

```c
InventoryNode* avl_new_node(Product product)
{
   InventoryNode* node = (InventoryNode*)malloc(sizeof(InventoryNode));
   if (node != NULL)
   {
      node->product = product;
      node->left = NULL;
      node->right = NULL;
      node->height = 1;
      return node;
   }
   else
   {
      printf("Error allocating memory. Exiting...");
      exit(1);
   }
}
```


Note that the height of the node is set to 1.

Next, we proceed with the definition of two functions for the rotation of the tree to the left or to the right:

```c
InventoryNode* avl_rotate_right(InventoryNode* y)
{
   printf("right rotate\n");
   InventoryNode* x = y->left;
   InventoryNode* T2 = x->right;

   x->right = y;
   y->left = T2;

   y->height = max(avl_get_height(y->left), avl_get_height(y->right)) + 1;
   x->height = max(avl_get_height(x->left), avl_get_height(x->right)) + 1;

   return x;
}

InventoryNode* avl_rotate_left(InventoryNode* x)
{
```

```c
    printf("left rotate\n");
    InventoryNode* y = x->right;
    InventoryNode* T2 = y->left;

    y->left = x;
    x->right = T2;

    x->height = max(avl_get_height(x->left), avl_get_height(x->right)) + 1;
    y->height = max(avl_get_height(y->left), avl_get_height(y->right)) + 1;

    return y;
}
```

Listing 14-4: inventoryAVL.c

Those two functions will be used when we will try to insert a new node into the tree:

```c
InventoryNode* avl_insert_node(InventoryNode* node, Product product)
{
  if (node == NULL)
    return avl_new_node(product);

  if (product.id < node->product.id)
    node->left = avl_insert_node(node->left, product);
  else if (product.id > node->product.id)
    node->right = avl_insert_node(node->right, product);
  else
    return node;

  node->height = 1 + max(avl_get_height(node->left), avl_get_height(node->right));

  int balance = avl_get_balance(node);

  if (balance > 1 && product.id < node->left->product.id)
    return avl_rotate_right(node);

  if (balance < -1 && product.id > node->right->product.id)
    return avl_rotate_left(node);

  if (balance > 1 && product.id > node->left->product.id)
  {
    node->left = avl_rotate_left(node->left);
    return avl_rotate_right(node);
  }

  if (balance < -1 && product.id < node->right->product.id)
  {
    node->right = avl_rotate_right(node->right);
    return avl_rotate_left(node);
  }

  return node;
}
```

Listing 14-5: inventoryAVL.c

Next, we present the functions to traverse the tree while printing its contents, as well as the code to search for a specific product in the tree:

```c
void avl_traverse_tree(InventoryNode* root)
{
  if (root != NULL)
  {
    avl_traverse_tree(root->left);
    printf("ID: %d, Name: %s, Price: %.2f, Quantity: %d\n", root->product.id,
      root->product.name, root->product.price, root->product.quantity);
    avl_traverse_tree(root->right);
  }
}

InventoryNode* avl_search_product(InventoryNode* root, int id)
{
  if (root == NULL || root->product.id == id)
  {
    if (root == NULL)
      printf("Product not found.\n");
    else
      printf("Product found:\nID: %d, Name: %s, Price: %.2f, Quantity: %d\n",
        root->product.id, root->product.name,
        root->product.price, root->product.quantity);
    return root;
  }

  printf("Visited product ID: %d\n", root->product.id);

  if (id < root->product.id)
    return avl_search_product(root->left, id);
  else
    return avl_search_product(root->right, id);
}
```


Traversing the tree means visiting each node in the tree, and this is performed recursively, first for the left branch and then for the right branch.

Searching for a product in the tree works in similar fashion: we visit a node, and we check the product's ID. If it matches the search ID, then we print the product details and the function returns. Otherwise, we visit the left or the right branch of the tree recursively, depending on the search ID.

Finally, here is the `main()` function:

```c
int main()
{
  InventoryNode* root = NULL;
  Product products[100];

  // Adding 100 random products
```

```c
  srand((unsigned int)time(NULL));
  for (int i = 0; i < 100; i++)
  {
    products[i].id = i + 1;
    sprintf(products[i].name, "Product %d", products[i].id);
    products[i].price = (float)(rand() % 1000) / 10.0;
    products[i].quantity = rand() % 100 + 1;
  }

  // Shuffle the array of products
  srand((unsigned int)time(NULL));
  for (int i = 99; i > 0; i--)
  {
    int j = rand() % (i + 1);
    Product temp = products[i];
    products[i] = products[j];
    products[j] = temp;
  }

  for (int i = 0; i < 100; i++)
  {
    root = avl_insert_node(root, products[i]);
  }

  // Print inventory
  printf("Inventory:\n");
  avl_traverse_tree(root);

  // Search for a product
  int productIdToSearch = 35;
  InventoryNode* foundProduct = avl_search_product(root, productIdToSearch);
  if (foundProduct != NULL)
  {
    printf("Product found:\n");
    printf("ID: %d, Name: %s, Price: %.2f, Quantity: %d\n",
      foundProduct->product.id, foundProduct->product.name,
      foundProduct->product.price, foundProduct->product.quantity);
  }
  else
  {
    printf("Product with ID %d not found.\n", productIdToSearch);
  }
  return 0;
}
```

Listing 14-7: inventoryAVL.c

We create 100 products with random quantities and prices and place them in an array.
Then we shuffle the array in a random order. Afterwards, we insert the products into the
AVL tree and we print its contents. Finally, a search is performed for a specific product ID.
During the search process we print the visited nodes to get an idea of how fast we will find
the specific ID inside the AVL tree.

You can find this project in GitHub:

https://github.com/htset/advanced_c_exercises/tree/master/InventoryAVL

15. Hotel Reservations

In this exercise, we will create an application that will handle reservations in apartments (in AirBnB style).

We need to manage the following information:

Apartments:

- Address
- Capacity (maximum persons)
- Price per day

Reservations:
- Name and surname of the person who made the reservation
- Start date
- Duration
- A list of the persons that will stay. For the persons, we will need to have:
  - Name and surname
  - Birth year

We will store all the information inside a MySQL database. We will also create a console-based UI that will handle the following operations:

- Adding a new reservation
- Search for a reservation based on the person's surname
- List all reservations

For simplicity, we will not handle the apartments in the UI. They will be inserted with SQL directly into the Apartments table. Also, we will not care about booking the same apartment more than one time, just to keep the implementation easy to follow.

Proposed Solution

We start with the definition of the database tables. We will use MySQL for this exercise, as it has the most straightforward API to be used even by novice programmers.

Here is the SQL for the creation of the tables:

```sql
CREATE DATABASE `test`;

CREATE TABLE `apartments` (
  `id` int NOT NULL AUTO_INCREMENT,
  `address` varchar(45) DEFAULT NULL,
  `capacity` int DEFAULT NULL,
  `price` int DEFAULT NULL,
  PRIMARY KEY (`id`)
) ENGINE=InnoDB AUTO_INCREMENT=3 DEFAULT CHARSET=utf8mb4 COLLATE=utf8mb4_0900_ai_ci;
```

```sql
CREATE TABLE `reservations` (
  `id` int NOT NULL AUTO_INCREMENT,
  `name` varchar(45) DEFAULT NULL,
  `surname` varchar(45) DEFAULT NULL,
  `start_date` date DEFAULT NULL,
  `duration` int DEFAULT NULL,
  `cost` decimal(10,2) DEFAULT NULL,
  PRIMARY KEY (`id`)
) ENGINE=InnoDB AUTO_INCREMENT=8 DEFAULT CHARSET=utf8mb4 COLLATE=utf8mb4_0900_ai_ci;

CREATE TABLE `persons` (
  `id` int NOT NULL AUTO_INCREMENT,
  `name` varchar(45) DEFAULT NULL,
  `surname` varchar(45) DEFAULT NULL,
  `birth_year` int DEFAULT NULL,
  `reservation_id` int DEFAULT NULL,
  PRIMARY KEY (`id`)
) ENGINE=InnoDB AUTO_INCREMENT=5 DEFAULT CHARSET=utf8mb4 COLLATE=utf8mb4_0900_ai_ci;
```

Listing 15-1: SQL code

We can use the MySQL Workbench application to create the database and the corresponding tables.

To connect with the database, we will use the MySQL C API, which comes with the installation of the MySQL database. We need to add references to the include files and libraries for the MySQL C API.

Let's see how to do it for Visual Studio projects: We open the Project Properties page and in the "C/C++ → General" page we have to add the MySQL include folder in the "Additional Include Directories" text box:

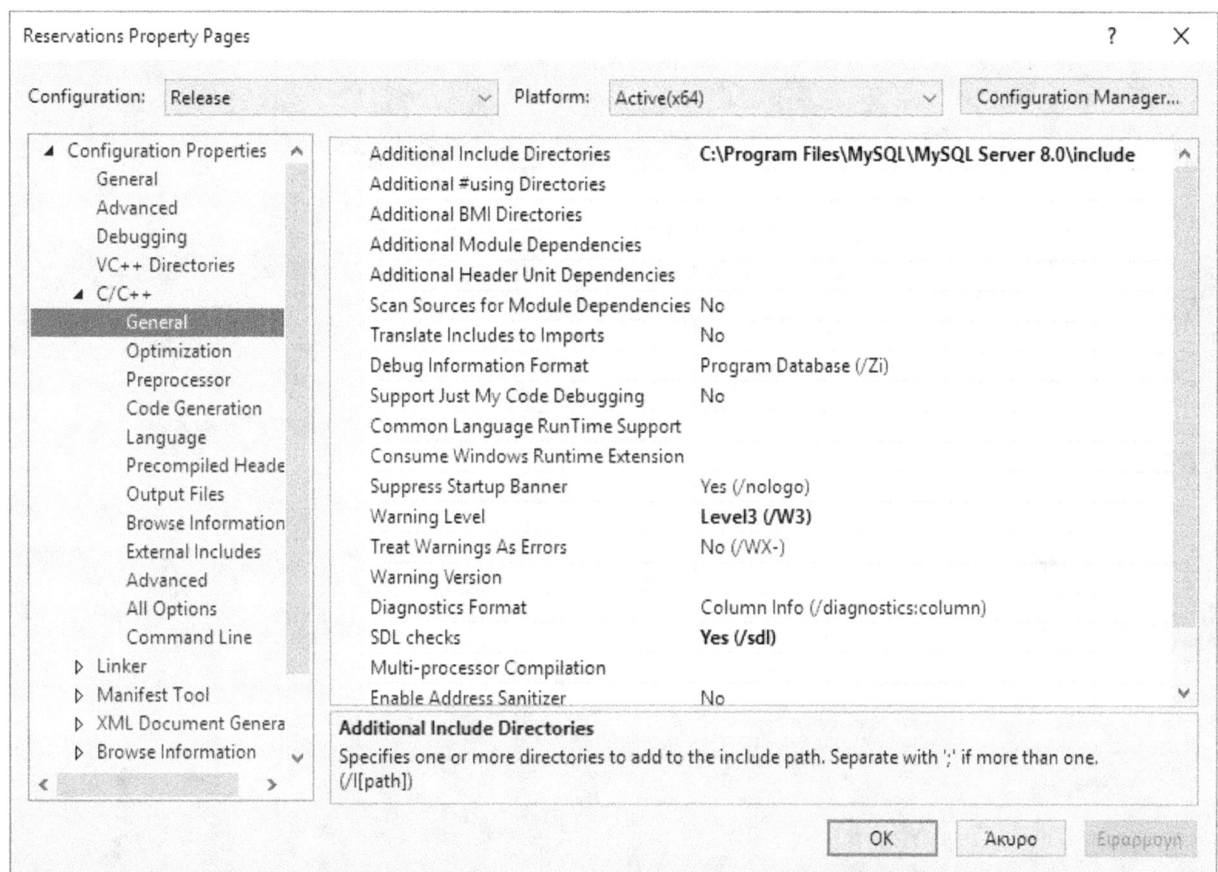

Also, in the "Linker → General" page, we add the MySQL library folder in the "Additional Library Directories" text box:

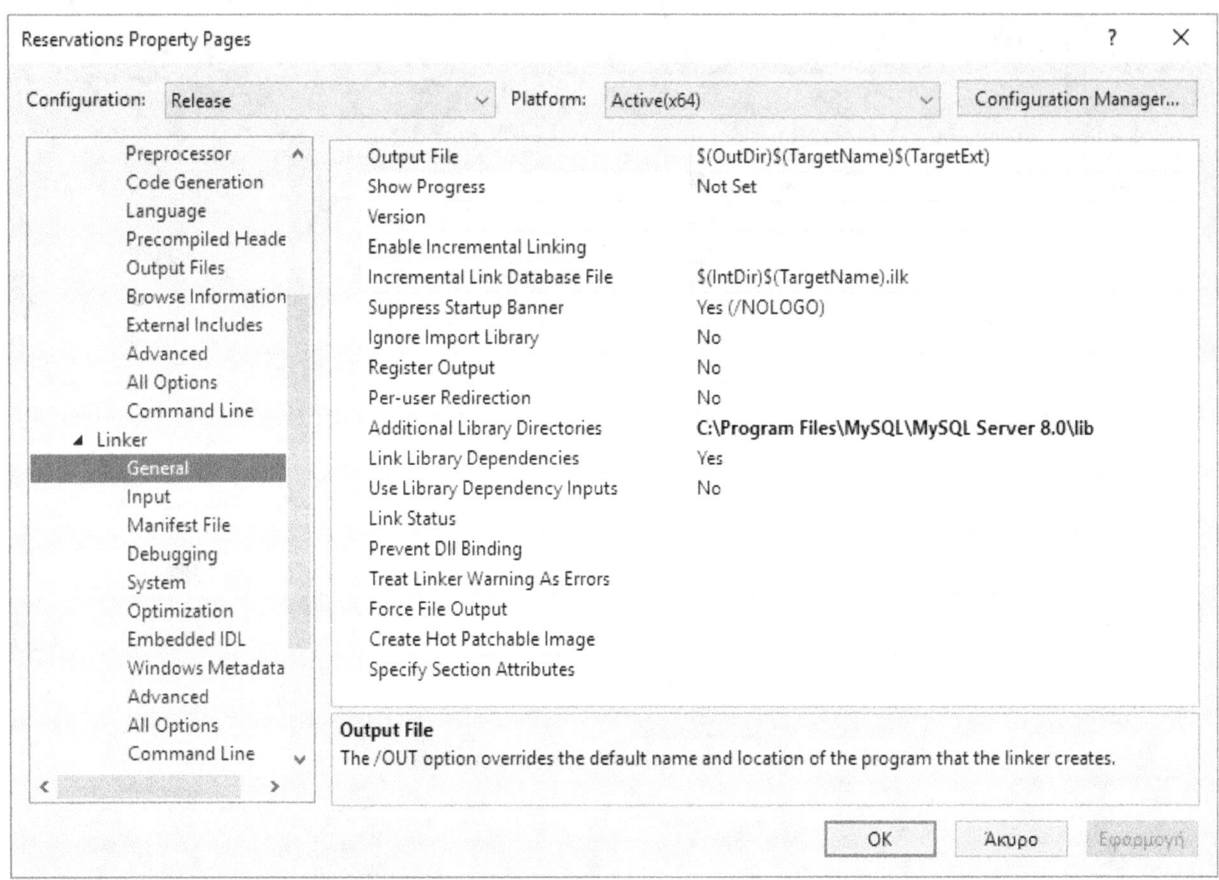

One last addition is in "Linker → Input", where we specify "libmysql.lib" in "Additional Dependencies":

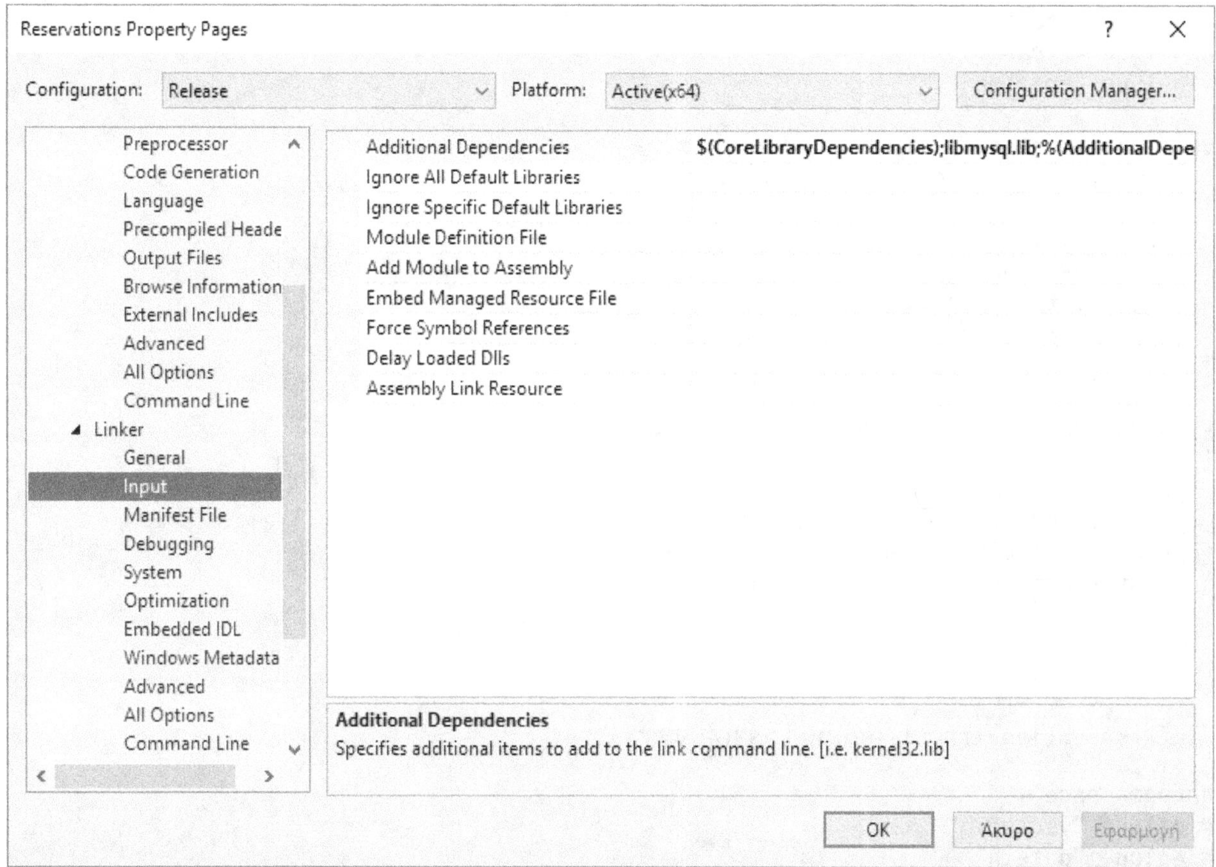

Finally, we have to copy the corresponding DLL (*libmysql.dll*) to the executable file directory.

Now we are ready setup-wise, so let's proceed to the code: first we define the Apartment struct:

```
#pragma once
struct Apartment
{
  int id;
  char address[100];
  int capacity;
  double price;
};

void apartment_set(struct Apartment* a,
  int id, char* address, int capacity, double price);
void apartment_print(struct Apartment* a);
```

Listing 15-2: apartment.h

Here we use the #pragma once directive to ensure that the file is included only once during compilation, thus preventing multiple definitions of the same entities.

Here is the implementation of the respective functions:

```c
#include <stdio.h>
#include <string.h>
#include "apartment.h"

void apartment_set(struct Apartment* a,
  int id, char* address, int capacity, double price)
{
  a->id = id;
  strcpy(a->address, address);
  a->capacity = capacity;
  a->price = price;
}

void apartment_print(struct Apartment *a)
{
  printf("ID: %d\n", a->id);
  printf("Address: %s\n", a->address) ;
  printf("Capacity: %d\n", a->capacity);
  printf("Price: %f\n", a->price);
}
```

Listing 15-3: apartment.c

The Reservation struct is defined as follows:

```c
#pragma once
#include "vector.h"
#include "date.h"
#include "person.h"

struct Reservation
{
  int id;
  char name[100];
  char surname[100];
  struct Date start_date;
  int duration;
  double cost;
  struct Vector persons;
};

void reservation_add_person(struct Reservation* r, struct Person p);
void reservation_set(struct Reservation* r,
  int id, char* name, char* surname,
  struct Date start_date, int duration, double cost);
void reservation_print(struct Reservation* resv);
```

Listing 15-4: reservation.h

Here is the implementation of the declared functions:

```c
#include "reservation.h"

void reservation_add_person(struct Reservation* r, struct Person p)
{
```

```c
    vector_push_back(&r->persons, p);
}

void reservation_set(struct Reservation* r,
    int id, char* name, char* surname,
    struct Date start_date, int duration, double cost)
{
    r->id = id;
    strcpy(r->name, name);
    strcpy(r->surname, surname);
    r->start_date = start_date;
    r->duration = duration;
    r->cost = cost;
    vector_init(&r->persons, 5);
}

void reservation_print(struct Reservation *resv)
{
    printf("ID: %d\n", resv->id);
    printf("Name: %s\n", resv->name);
    printf("Surname: %s\n", resv->surname);
    printf("Start Date: ");
    date_print(&resv->start_date);
    printf("\nDuration: %d\n", resv->duration);
    printf("Cost: %.2f\n", resv->cost);
}
```


The Reservation class contains a list of the persons that will stay in the apartment. This list is a vector implementation that handles Person objects. Let's see the Person struct first:

```c
#pragma once
struct Person
{
    int id;
    char name[100];
    char surname[100];
    int birth_year;
};

void person_set(struct Person* p,
    int id, char* name, char* surname, int birth_year);
void person_print(struct Person* p);
```


And the implementation of the functions:

```c
#include <stdio.h>
#include <string.h>
#include "person.h"

void person_set(struct Person *p,
```

```c
  int id, char* name, char* surname, int birth_year)
{
  p->id = id;
  strcpy(p->name, name);
  strcpy(p->surname, surname);
  p->birth_year = birth_year;
}

void person_print(struct Person* p)
{
  printf("ID: %d\n", p->id);
  printf("Name: %s\n", p->name);
  printf("Surname: %s\n", p->surname);
  printf("Birth Year: %d\n", p->birth_year);
}
```

Listing 15-7: person.c

Now, let's see the definition of the Vector struct:

```c
#pragma once
#include <stdio.h>
#include <stdlib.h>
#include "person.h"

struct Vector
{
  struct Person* persons;
  size_t size;
  size_t capacity;
} ;

void vector_init(struct Vector* vec, size_t capacity);
void vector_push_back(struct Vector* vec, struct Person value);
struct Person vector_at(const struct Vector* vec, size_t index);
void vector_free(struct Vector* vec);
```

Listing 15-8: vector.h

Here is the implementation. The specifics of the Vector class have been analysed in a previous exercise:

```c
#include "vector.h"

void vector_init(struct Vector* vec, size_t capacity)
{
  vec->persons = (struct Person*)malloc(capacity * sizeof(struct Person));
  if (vec->persons == NULL)
  {
    printf("Memory allocation failed\n");
    exit(1);
  }
  vec->size = 0;
  vec->capacity = capacity;
```

```c
}

void vector_push_back(struct Vector* vec, struct Person value)
{
  if (vec->size >= vec->capacity)
  {
    vec->capacity *= 2;
    vec->persons = (struct Person*)realloc(vec->persons,
      vec->capacity * sizeof(struct Person));
    if (vec->persons == NULL)
    {
      printf("Memory allocation failed\n");
      exit(1);
    }
  }
  vec->persons[vec->size++] = value;
}

struct Person vector_at(const struct Vector* vec, size_t index)
{
  if (index >= vec->size)
  {
    printf("Array index out of bounds\n");
    exit(1);
  }
  return vec->persons[index];
}

void vector_free(struct Vector* vec)
{
  free(vec->persons);
  vec->persons = NULL;
  vec->size = 0;
  vec->capacity = 0;
}
```

Listing 15-9: vector.c

The Reservation struct also contains a Date struct, that keeps the reservation start date:

```c
#pragma once

struct Date
{
  int day;
  int month;
  int year;
};

void date_now(struct Date* d);
void date_set(struct Date* d, int _day, int _month, int _year);
void addDays(struct Date* d, int days);
char* date_serialize();
void deserialize(struct Date* d, char* s);
char* toMysqlDate(struct Date* d);
```

And the implementation:

```c
#include <time.h>
#include "Date.h"

void date_now(struct Date *d)
{
  time_t t = time(0);

  struct tm now;
  localtime_s(&now, &t);
  d->day = now.tm_mday;
  d->month = now.tm_mon + 1;
  d->year = now.tm_year + 1900;
}

void date_set(struct Date *d, int _day, int _month, int _year)
{
  d->day = _day;
  d->month = _month;
  d->year = _year;
}

void addDays(struct Date *d, int days)
{
  struct tm tmp;
  tmp.tm_mday = d->day;
  tmp.tm_mon = d->month - 1;
  tmp.tm_year = d->year - 1900;
  time_t now = mktime(&tmp);

  time_t newSeconds = now + days * (60 * 60 * 24);
  struct tm newDate;
  localtime_s(&newDate, &newSeconds);

  d->day = newDate.tm_mday;
  d->month = newDate.tm_mon + 1;
  d->year = newDate.tm_year + 1900;
}

void date_print(struct Date* d)
{
  printf("%d/%d/%d", d->day, d->month, d->year);
}
```


Now, let's see the functions that handle the user interface. The add_persons() function is used to get the guests data from the user:

```c
#include "db.h"
```

```c
#include "apartment.h"
#include "reservation.h"
#include "date.h"
#include "person.h"

void add_persons(struct Reservation* resv)
{
  char name[100], surname[100];
  int birth_year;
  char option;

  printf("Give the persons:\n");
  do
  {
    printf("Name: ");
    fgets(name, sizeof(name), stdin);
    name[strcspn(name, "\n")] = '\0';

    printf("Surname: ");
    fgets(surname, sizeof(surname), stdin);
    surname[strcspn(surname, "\n")] = '\0';

    printf("Birth Year: ");
    scanf("%d", &birth_year);
    getchar();

    struct Person p;
    person_set(&p, 0, name, surname, birth_year);

    reservation_add_person(resv, p);

    printf("Add another person? (y/n)\n");
    scanf("%c", &option);
    getchar();
  } while (option != 'n' && option != 'N');
}
```


Note the use of the `strcspn()` function, in order to replace the trailing newline in the string with the string terminating character. For each guest, a new `struct Person` object is created and inserted into the vector in the reservation.

The `add_persons()` function is used by the `add_reservation()` function:

```c
void add_reservation()
{
  int option;
  char name[100], surname[100], startDateStr[100];
  int duration, day, month, year;

  printf("Name: ");
  fgets(name, sizeof(name), stdin);
  name[strcspn(name, "\n")] = '\0';
```

```c
printf("Surname: ");
fgets(surname, sizeof(surname), stdin);
surname[strcspn(surname, "\n")] = '\0';

printf("Start date: ");
fgets(startDateStr, sizeof(startDateStr), stdin);
startDateStr[strcspn(startDateStr, "\n")] = '\0';

sscanf(startDateStr, "%2d/%2d/%4d", &day, &month, &year);
struct Date startDate;
date_set(&startDate, day, month, year);

printf("Duration: ");
scanf("%d", &duration);
getchar();

printf("Available apartments:\n");
struct Apartment* apartments;
int count;
db_get_apartments(&apartments, &count);
for (int i = 0; i < count; i++)
{
  printf("Apartment no.%d\n", i + 1);
  apartment_print(&apartments[i]);
}
printf("Press 0 to cancel:");
scanf("%d", &option);
getchar();

if (option > 0 && option <= sizeof(apartments))
{
  struct Reservation resv;
  reservation_set(&resv, 0, name, surname, startDate, duration,
    apartments[option - 1].price);

  add_persons(&resv);

  db_insert_reservation(&resv);
}
}
```


After having entered the desired start date and duration of the reservation, the user is presented with a list of the available apartments. Normally, we would search for free apartments in those dates, but for simplicity we get all the apartments in the database. You should make sure you have instered some apartments int othe database, perhaps using the MySQL Workspace application.

The apartments list is retrieved with the use of the `db_get_apartments()` function. After selecting an apartment, the user is prompted to insert one by one all the persons that will stay in the apartment.

The `db_get_apartments()` function will fill up an array of the available Apartments and their total number (variable `count`). Note that we pass a double pointer (i.e., `struct Apartments**`) as input to the the function. This happens because we will need to allocate memory with `malloc()` inside this function, therefore we will need to set the value of the pointer (hence, we need to get a pointer to this pointer).

Moreover, we use the `sscanf()` function to parse the `startDateStr` string into the 3 integers (day, month and year). Note also the use of the `getchar()` function to remove the newline character that remains in the stdin stream.

After getting the input from the user, we create a new reservation object. Note that we provide 0 as the `id` of the reservation, as this value will be automatically generated by the MySQL database when we insert the new entry.

Next, we implement the case where we search for a specific reservation, by using the surname of the client:

```c
void search_reservation()
{
  char surname[100];
  printf("Enter surname (also partial): ");
  scanf("%s", surname);
  getchar();

  struct Reservation *resv;
  int count;
  db_get_reservations_by_surname(&resv, &count, surname);

  for (int i = 0; i < count; i++)
  {
    reservation_print(&resv[i]);
    printf("-------------\n");
  }
}
```

Listing 15-14: main.c

Here, we call the `db_get_reservations_by_surname()` function, in the same way as previously discussed.

Then, we have the case where we display all the inserted reservations:

```c
void list_reservations()
{
  struct Reservation* resv;
  int count;
  db_get_all_reservations(&resv, &count);
```

```c
  for (int i = 0; i < count; i++)
  {
    reservation_print(&resv[i]);
    printf("-------------\n");
  }
}
```


The menu() function contains the main loop of the interaction with the user:

```c
void menu()
{
  int option;
  do
  {
    printf("Options: \n");
    printf("1) Add reservation \n");
    printf("2) Search reservation \n");
    printf("3) View all reservations \n");
    printf("0) Exit \n");
    printf("Enter your selection:");
    scanf("%d", &option);
    getchar();

    switch (option)
    {
    case 1:
      add_reservation();
      break;
    case 2:
      search_reservation();
      break;
    case 3:
      list_reservations();
      break;
    case 0:
      break;
    default:
      printf("Please enter selection again:");
      break;
    }
  } while (option != 0);
}
```


The main function is very simple, as it initializes the database connection, calls the menu loop and at the end releases the database resources:

```c
int main()
{
  db_init();
```

```c
  menu();
  db_close();
}
```


Now, we turn to the database handling code:

```c
#pragma once
#include "date.h"
#include "reservation.h"
#include "apartment.h"

#include <mysql.h>

#define DEFAULT_URI "localhost"
#define EXAMPLE_USER "xxxxxx"
#define EXAMPLE_PASS "xxxxxx"
#define EXAMPLE_DB "test"

MYSQL* conn;

void db_init();
void db_close();
void db_get_apartments(struct Apartment** apartments, int* count);
void db_get_all_reservations(struct Reservation** reservations, int* count);
void db_get_reservations_by_surname(struct Reservation** reservations,
  int* count, char* surname);
void db_insert_reservation(struct Reservation* resv);
```


We put all the database functionality in a separate file, and we do not mix the code with the application logic. In this way, it will be easy to adapt our application to use a different database, as we will need only to write a new *db.c* file.

Let's see first the implementation of the initialization and release of the database connection:

```c
#include <stdio.h>
#include <string.h>
#include "db.h"

void error_exit(MYSQL* con)
{
  fprintf(stderr, "%s\n", mysql_error(con));
  mysql_close(con);
  exit(1);
}

void db_init()
{
  conn = mysql_init(NULL);
  mysql_autocommit(conn, 0);
```

```c
  if (conn == NULL)
  {
    fprintf(stderr, "mysql_init() failed\n");
    exit(1);
  }

  if (mysql_real_connect(conn, DEFAULT_URI,
    EXAMPLE_USER, EXAMPLE_PASS, EXAMPLE_DB, 0, NULL, 0) == NULL)
  {
    error_exit(conn);
  }
}

void db_close()
{
  mysql_close(conn);
}
```


Note that we disable *auto commit* for the database. This means that we will need to commit our changes in order to take effect in the database.

The `db_get_apartments()` function retrieves all apartments for the database:

```c
void db_get_apartments(struct Apartment** apartments, int* count)
{
  if (mysql_query(conn, "SELECT id, address, capacity, price from Apartments"))
  {
    error_exit(conn);
  }

  MYSQL_RES* result = mysql_store_result(conn);

  if (result == NULL)
  {
    error_exit(conn);
  }

  int num_fields = mysql_num_fields(result);
  *count = mysql_num_rows(result);
  *apartments = malloc((*count) * sizeof(struct Apartment));
  if (*apartments == NULL)
  {
    printf("Memory allocation error!\n");
    exit(1);
  }

  MYSQL_ROW row;
  int i = 0;
  while ((row = mysql_fetch_row(result)))
  {
    (*apartments)[i].id = atoi(row[0]);
```

```c
    strcpy((*apartments)[i].address, row[1]);
    (*apartments)[i].capacity = atoi(row[2]);
    (*apartments)[i].price = atof(row[3]);
    i++;
  }

  mysql_free_result(result);
}
```


After running the query, we can retrieve the total number of entries returned. We use this number in order to allocate memory for an array of struct Apartment objects.

Then, we loop over the entries. Each entry consists of an array of strings. We have to convert some of the strings into int and double with the atoi() and atof() function respectively.

The db_get_all_reservations() retrieves all the reservations in the database:

```c
void db_get_all_reservations(struct Reservation** reservations, int *count)
{
  if (mysql_query(conn, "SELECT id, name, surname, start_date, duration, cost from Reservations"))
  {
    error_exit(conn);
  }

  MYSQL_RES* result = mysql_store_result(conn);

  if (result == NULL)
  {
    error_exit(conn);
  }

  int num_fields = mysql_num_fields(result);
  *count = mysql_num_rows(result);
  *reservations = malloc((*count) * sizeof(struct Reservation));
  if (*reservations == NULL)
  {
    printf("Memory allocation error!\n");
    exit(1);
  }

  MYSQL_ROW row;
  int i = 0;
  while ((row = mysql_fetch_row(result)))
  {
    (*reservations)[i].id = atoi(row[0]);
    strcpy((*reservations)[i].name, row[1]);
    strcpy((*reservations)[i].surname, row[2]);

    char* ptr = strtok((char*)row[3], "-");
    int year = atoi(ptr);
```

```c
    ptr = strtok(NULL, "-");
    int month = atoi(ptr);
    ptr = strtok(NULL, "-");
    int day = atoi(ptr);
    date_set(&((*reservations)[i].start_date), day, month, year);

    (*reservations)[i].duration = atoi(row[4]);
    (*reservations)[i].cost = atof(row[5]);
    i++;
  }

  mysql_free_result(result);
}
```


Here, we need to have some processing to get the `struct Date` object from the database. We will use the `strtok()` tokenizing function. We use `strtok()` in 3 successive calls to split the date string by the dash(-) sign. Note that we only pass the initial date string in the first function call; in the other 2 calls we pass NULL.

The `db_get_reservations_by_surname()` function returns a list of reservations for a specific surname:

```c
void db_get_reservations_by_surname(struct Reservation** reservations, int* count,
char* surname)
{
  char query[1000];
  sprintf(query, "SELECT id, name, surname, start_date, duration, cost from
Reservations where surname like '%%%s%%'", surname);
  if (mysql_query(conn, query))
  {
    error_exit(conn);
  }

  MYSQL_RES* result = mysql_store_result(conn);

  if (result == NULL)
  {
    error_exit(conn);
  }

  int num_fields = mysql_num_fields(result);
  *count = mysql_num_rows(result);
  *reservations = malloc((*count) * sizeof(struct Reservation));
  if (*reservations == NULL)
  {
    printf("Memory allocation error!\n");
    exit(1);
  }

  MYSQL_ROW row;
  int i = 0;
```

```c
while ((row = mysql_fetch_row(result)))
{
  (*reservations)[i].id = atoi(row[0]);
  strcpy((*reservations)[i].name, row[1]);
  strcpy((*reservations)[i].surname, row[2]);

  char* ptr = strtok((char*)row[3], "-");
  int year = atoi(ptr);
  ptr = strtok(NULL, "-");
  int month = atoi(ptr);
  ptr = strtok(NULL, "-");
  int day = atoi(ptr);
  date_set(&((*reservations)[i].start_date), day, month, year);

  (*reservations)[i].duration = atoi(row[4]);
  (*reservations)[i].cost = atof(row[5]);
  i++;
}

  mysql_free_result(result);
}
```


Inside the SQL query we use the LIKE clause along with the % sign. Note that we have to escape the % sign with another percentage sign (i.e., %%).

Finally, we also have a function to insert a new reservation (and the corresponding persons) in the database:

```c
void db_insert_reservation(struct Reservation* resv)
{
  char query[1000];
  char date[20];
  sprintf(date, "%d-%d-%d", resv->start_date.year, resv->start_date.month, resv->start_date.day);
  sprintf(query, "insert into Reservations(name, surname, start_date, duration, cost) values('%s','%s','%s',%d,%f)",
    resv->name, resv->surname, date, resv->duration, resv->cost);

  if(mysql_query(conn, query))
  {
    mysql_rollback(conn);
    error_exit(conn);
  }

  int id = mysql_insert_id(conn);

  for (int i = 0; i < resv->persons.size; i++)
  {
    sprintf(query, "insert into Persons(name, surname, birth_year, reservation_id) values('%s', '%s', %d, %d)",
      vector_at(&resv->persons, i).name, vector_at(&resv->persons, i).surname,
      vector_at(&resv->persons, i).birth_year, id);
```

```c
    if (mysql_query(conn, query))
    {
      mysql_rollback(conn);
      error_exit(conn);
    }
  }

  mysql_commit(conn);
  printf("Reservation inserted successfully!\n\n");
}
```

Listing 15-23: db.c

In db_insert_reservation() we first insert a new row in the Reservations table. The id field of the reservation is created automatically by the database, as we have defined it as AUTO_INCREMENT during the creation of the table.

Upon successful insertion of the row, we get newly generated reservation id, because we need to use it in each new Persons row (in the reservation_id field).

We perform successive inserts, one for each person, and at the end we commit our changes. In case of an exception, we can rollback the transaction and return to where we started.

You can find this project in GitHub:

https://github.com/htset/advanced_c_exercises/tree/master/Reservations

16. Pacman Game

In this exercise we will create a PacMan game with character-based graphics.

Proposed Solution

First of all, we define the game map:

```c
#pragma once
#include "entity.h"

enum BlockType { Wall, Point, Empty };

struct Pair{
  int x;
  int y;
};

struct Block
{
  enum BlockType type;
  struct Entity* entity;
};

struct Game
{
  struct Block map[32][28];
  int sizeX;
  int sizeY;
  int gameActive;
  struct Pair pacmanLocation;
  int pointsLeft;
};

void init_game(struct Game* map);
void print_game(struct Game* map);
```

Listing 16-1: map.h

First, we define a `Pair` struct that will be handy with handling positions in the maze.

Next, we define a `Block` struct, which represents a block in the maze. Each block can be:

- A wall
- A space with a point
- An empty space

The entities of the game (*Pacman* and the *Ghosts*) can move to spaces, either empty or with points. When an entity moves to a block, then the `entity` pointer inside the Block object will be set to point to the entity object.

Moreover, the `Map` class defines a fixed-sized array of `Block` objects. It also manages the position of the `Pacman` object in the maze (we could also get it by searching the blocks one by one, but this is more costly).

Here is the implementation of the functions:

```c
#include <stdio.h>
#include <string.h>
#include <stdlib.h>
#include "map.h"
#include "entity.h"

char* chart[32] =
{
"****************************",
"*............**............*",
"*.****.*****.**.*****.****.*",
"*.****.*****.**.*****.****.*",
"*.****.*****.**.*****.****.*",
"*..........................*",
"*.****.**.********.**.****.*",
"*.****.**.********.**.****.*",
"*......**....**....**......*",
"******.***** ** *****.******",
"******.***** ** *****.******",
"******.**          **.******",
"******.**.********.**.******",
"******.**.********.**.******",
"*     .   ********   .     *",
"******.**.********.**.******",
"******.**.********.**.******",
"******.**          **.******",
"******.**.********.**.******",
"******.**.********.**.******",
"*............**............*",
"*.****.*****.**.*****.****.*",
"*.****.*****.**.*****.****.*",
"*...**................**...*",
"***.**.**.********.**.**.***",
"***.**.**.********.**.**.***",
"*...**.**....**....**.**...*",
"*.**********.**.**********.*",
"*.**********....**********.*",
"*..........................*",
"****************************"
};

void init_game(struct Game* game)
{
    game->sizeX = 32;
    game->sizeY = 28;
    game->gameActive = 1;
```

```c
  game->pointsLeft = 0;
  for (int i = 0; i < 32; i++)
  {
    char* line = chart[i];
    for (int j = 0; j < 28; j++)
    {
      game->map[i][j].entity = NULL;

      if (line[j] == '.')
      {
        game->map[i][j].type = Point;
        game->pointsLeft++;
      }
      else if (line[j] == '*')
        game->map[i][j].type = Wall;
      if (line[j] == ' ')
        game->map[i][j].type = Empty;
    }
  }
}

void print_game(struct Game* game)
{
  char output[1000];
  memset(output, 0, 1000);
  system("cls");
  for (int i = 0; i < 32; i++)
  {
    for (int j = 0; j < 28; j++)
    {
      if (game->map[i][j].entity != NULL)
      {
        if(game->map[i][j].entity->type == Pacman)
          strcat(output, "C");
        else if (game->map[i][j].entity->type == Ghost)
          strcat(output, "A");
      }
      else
      {
        if (game->map[i][j].type == Wall)
          strcat(output, "*");
        else if (game->map[i][j].type == Point)
          strcat(output, ".");
        else if (game->map[i][j].type == Empty)
          strcat(output, " ");
      }
    }
    strcat(output, "\n");
  }
  printf(output);
}
```

Listing 16-2: map.c

During the initialization of the game, we parse an array of strings that make up a text representation of the maze. The asterisks denote a wall, while the dots represent spaces with points. Finally, there are some empty spaces denoted with the space symbol.

The `print_game()` function is called during every loop and prints the map in the console, along with the entities that roam it.

Speaking about the loop, let's see its implementation in the *main.c* file:

```c
#include <Windows.h>
#include "entity.h"
#include "map.h"

int main()
{
  int exit = 0;
  struct Game game;
  init_game(&game);

  struct Entity entity[4];

  entity[0].type = Pacman;
  entity[0].x = 23;
  entity[0].y = 13;
  game.map[23][13].entity = &entity[0];

  entity[1].type = Ghost;
  entity[1].x = 5;
  entity[1].y = 5;
  game.map[5][5].entity = &entity[1];

  entity[2].type = Ghost;
  entity[2].x = 5;
  entity[2].y = 20;
  game.map[5][20].entity = &entity[2];

  entity[3].type = Ghost;
  entity[3].x = 8;
  entity[3].y = 5;
  game.map[8][5].entity = &entity[3];

  int counter = 0;
  while (game.gameActive == 1 && exit != 1)
  {
    if (GetAsyncKeyState(VK_UP) & 0x8000)
      entity[0].direction = Up;
    if (GetAsyncKeyState(VK_RIGHT) & 0x8000)
      entity[0].direction = Right;
    if (GetAsyncKeyState(VK_DOWN) & 0x8000)
      entity[0].direction = Down;
    if (GetAsyncKeyState(VK_LEFT) & 0x8000)
      entity[0].direction = Left;
```

```c
    if (GetKeyState(VK_SPACE) & 0x8000)
    {
      exit = 1;
    }

    Sleep(20);

    if (counter++ > 10)
    {
      counter = 0;
      play_pacman(&entity[0], &game);
      play_ghost(&entity[1], &game);
      play_ghost(&entity[2], &game);
      play_ghost(&entity[3], &game);

      print_game(&game);
    }
  }
}
```

Listing 16-3: main.c

In `main()`, we first create the maze, as well as one Pacman and three Ghost objects. The newly created entities are placed in the map.

After the game setup, we start with the loop. The application sleeps for 20 ms in each loop and when it comes back it checks with the console whether the user has pressed any of the arrow keys. In this case, we update the direction of the Pacman entity (Pacman moves to one direction until it stumbles on a wall; then it stops).

After 10 iterations of the loop, every entity makes its move. We call the `play_pacman()` and `play_ghost()` functions, so that the next move is calculated. Finally, we print the new version of the map as it was updated after the moves.

The reason for the short intervals of each iteration (20 ms) is because we want to make the game responsive to user input. Longer sleep times would not allow the game to get correctly the key pressed by the user.

Now, let's see the `Entity` struct definition:

```c
#pragma once
#include "map.h"

enum Direction { Up, Right, Down, Left };
enum EntityType { Pacman, Ghost };

struct Entity
{
  int x;
  int y;
  enum Direction direction;
  enum EntityType type;
```

```c
};

void entity_move(struct Entity* entity, struct Game* map, int newX, int newY);
void play_pacman(struct Entity* pacman, struct Game* map);
void play_ghost(struct Entity* ghost, struct Game* map);
```


In this struct, we define the position (parameters x and y), the `direction` the entity is moving to and its `type` (`Pacman` or `Ghost`). We also define one function called `move()` that is used to move an entity inside the map.

Furthermore, we define the two functions that will be used to calculate the next position of the Pacman and Ghost entities.

In *entity.c* we have the implementation of those functions:

```c
#include <Math.h>
#include "entity.h"
#include "vector.h"

int find_min_distance_index(struct Vector* vec, struct Pair* pacmanCoords)
{
  int index = 0;
  double min_dist =
      sqrt(pow(vec->pair[0].x - pacmanCoords->x, 2) + pow(vec->pair[0].y -
pacmanCoords->y, 2));
  double temp_dist = 0;

  for (int i = 0; i < vec->size; i++)
  {
    temp_dist =
        sqrt(pow(vec->pair[i].x - pacmanCoords->x, 2) + pow(vec->pair[i].y -
pacmanCoords->y, 2));
    if (temp_dist < min_dist)
      index = i;
  }
  return index;
}

void entity_move(struct Entity* entity, struct Game* game, int newX, int newY)
{
  if (newX == entity->x && newY == entity->y)
    printf("error");

  game->map[newX][newY].entity
    = game->map[entity->x][entity->y].entity;

  game->map[entity->x][entity->y].entity = NULL;
  entity->x = newX;
  entity->y = newY;
}

void play_pacman(struct Entity* pacman, struct Game *game)
```

```c
{
  struct Vector candidateBlocks;
  int x = pacman->x;
  int y = pacman->y;

  vector_init(&candidateBlocks, 10);

  for (int i = x - 1; i <= x + 1; i++)
    for (int j = y - 1; j <= y + 1; j++)
    {
      if (i >= 0 && i < game->sizeX
        && j >= 0 && j < game->sizeY
        && !(i == x && j == y)
        && game->map[i][j].type != Wall)
      {
        struct Pair newPair;
        newPair.x = i;
        newPair.y = j;
        vector_push_back(&candidateBlocks, newPair);
      }
    }

  if (pacman->direction == Up
    && vector_contains_pair(&candidateBlocks, x - 1, y))
  {
    entity_move(pacman, game, x - 1, y);
  }
  else if (pacman->direction == Right
    && vector_contains_pair(&candidateBlocks, x, y + 1))
  {
    entity_move(pacman, game, x, y + 1);
  }
  else if (pacman->direction == Down
    && vector_contains_pair(&candidateBlocks, x + 1, y))
  {
    entity_move(pacman, game, x + 1, y);
  }
  else if (pacman->direction == Left
    && vector_contains_pair(&candidateBlocks, x, y - 1))
  {
    entity_move(pacman, game, x, y - 1);
  }
  game->pacmanLocation.x = x;
  game->pacmanLocation.y = y;

  if (game->map[x][y].type == Point)
  {
    game->map[x][y].type = Empty;
    game->pointsLeft--;
    if (game->pointsLeft == 0)
      game->gameActive = 0;
  }
}
```

```c
void play_ghost(struct Entity* ghost, struct  Game* game)
{
  struct Vector candidateBlocks;
  int x = ghost->x;
  int y = ghost->y;

  vector_init(&candidateBlocks, 10);

  for (int i = x - 1; i <= x + 1; i++)
    for (int j = y - 1; j <= y + 1; j++)
    {
      if (i >= 0 && i < game->sizeX
        && j >= 0 && j < game->sizeY
        && !(i == x && j == y)
        && game->map[i][j].type != Wall)
      {
        struct Pair newPair;
        newPair.x = i;
        newPair.y = j;
        vector_push_back(&candidateBlocks, newPair);
      }
    }

  int index = find_min_distance_index(&candidateBlocks, &game->pacmanLocation);

  if (game->map[vector_at(&candidateBlocks, index).x][vector_at(&candidateBlocks,
index).y].entity != NULL)
  {
    //move only if pacman is there
    if (game->map[vector_at(&candidateBlocks, index).x][vector_at(&candidateBlocks,
index).y].entity->type == Pacman)
    {
      //eat pacman
      game->map[vector_at(&candidateBlocks, index).x][vector_at(&candidateBlocks,
index).y].entity = NULL;
      game->gameActive = 0;
      entity_move(ghost, game, vector_at(&candidateBlocks, index).x,
vector_at(&candidateBlocks, index).y);
    }
  }
  else
  {
    entity_move(ghost, game, vector_at(&candidateBlocks, index).x,
vector_at(&candidateBlocks, index).y);
  }
}
```


The interesting stuff lies in the implementation of the `play_pacman()` function. First of all, we find all neighbouring blocks that `Pacman` can move to (that are not a wall actually) and we put them in a vector of *candidate blocks*.

Next, depending on the `direction` selected by the user (using the arrow buttons) we move Pacman into the respective block, if available. Moving Pacman into a block means also updating the map with the position of Pacman, as well the elimination of the point (if any) remaining in this block. The latter is performed by changing the type of the block to `Empty` and by reducing by one the remaining points in the game. If the points become zero (Pacman has eaten all the points), then the game comes to an end.

Even more interesting is the `play_ghost()` function, as the ghosts need to calculate a move closer to Pacman. Here, we again find the candidate neighbouring blocks for a move. Moreover, we calculate an array of the straight-line distances of each candidate position to the PacMan entity.

Then, we use the `find_min_distance_index()` function to find the index inside the vector, that contains the candidate block with the shortest distance to Pacman. Then, the Ghost will move to the block that is nearest to Pacman, in an effort to get closer to it.

A Ghost may not move in a block where there is another Ghost, but it can step into the block where Pacman is located. In this case, Pacman is eaten by the Ghost and the game comes to an end.

This game has definitively lots more to be done. For instance, we have to implement the mode change where Pacman starts chasing the Ghosts for a short period of time. A major enhancement would be to introduce graphics, something that would definitively make the game more beautiful and performant.

Finally, we present the code for the Vector struct, which is similar to the ones used in previous exercises:

```c
#pragma once
#include <stdio.h>
#include <stdlib.h>
#include "entity.h"

struct Vector{
    struct Pair* pair;
    size_t size;
    size_t capacity;
};

void vector_init(struct Vector* vec, size_t capacity);
void vector_push_back(struct Vector* vec, struct Pair value);
struct Pair vector_at(const struct Vector* vec, size_t index);
void vector_free(struct Vector* vec);
int vector_contains_pair(struct Vector* vec, int x, int y);
```

Listing 16-6: vector.h

And the implementation:

```c
#include "vector.h"

void vector_init(struct Vector* vec, size_t capacity)
{
  vec->pair = (struct Pair*)malloc(capacity * sizeof(struct Pair));
  if (vec->pair == NULL)
  {
    printf("Memory allocation failed\n");
    exit(1);
  }
  vec->size = 0;
  vec->capacity = capacity;
}

void vector_push_back(struct Vector* vec, struct Pair value)
{
  if (vec->size >= vec->capacity)
  {
    vec->capacity *= 2;
    vec->pair = (struct Pair*)realloc(vec->pair, vec->capacity * sizeof(struct
Pair));
    if (vec->pair == NULL)
    {
      printf("Memory allocation failed\n");
      exit(1);
    }
  }
  vec->pair[vec->size++] = value;
}

struct Pair vector_at(const struct Vector* vec, size_t index)
{
  if (index >= vec->size)
  {
    printf("Array index out of bounds\n");
    exit(1);
  }
  return vec->pair[index];
}

void vector_free(struct Vector* vec)
{
  free(vec->pair);
  vec->pair = NULL;
  vec->size = 0;
  vec->capacity = 0;
}

int vector_contains_pair(struct Vector* vec, int x, int y)
{
  for (int i = 0; i < vec->size; i++)
  {
```

```c
    struct Pair pair = vec->pair[i];
    if (pair.x == x && pair.y == y)
      return 1;
  }

  return 0;
}
```


You can find this project in GitHub:

https://github.com/htset/advanced_c_exercises/tree/master/Pacman

17. MNIST Image Comparison

In this exercise, we will play with handwriting images from the MNIST database.

Proposed Solution

The MNIST database (http://yann.lecun.com/exdb/mnist/) is a set of images depicting handwritten digits. The images are of 28x28 dimension and are typically used when studying pattern recognition and machine learning techniques.

Source: Wikipedia

We will download the following file and we will unzip it in our project's directory:

http://yann.lecun.com/exdb/mnist/train-images-idx3-ubyte.gz

We will also rename it as *input.dat*.

The first 15 bytes of this file, contain metadata about the images, i.e. the number of the images and their dimensions. Therefore, we will start reading from the 16th byte in steps of 28x28=784 bytes.

First, we define the `Image` struct that will store the image data in an array of `unsigned chars`:

```
#include <stdio.h>
#include <stdlib.h>
#include <math.h>
#include <time.h>
```

```c
#define IMAGE_SIZE 784     // Size of each image (28x28)
#define META_DATA_SIZE 15 // Size of meta data at the beginning of the file

// Structure to represent an image
typedef struct Image
{
  unsigned char pixels[IMAGE_SIZE]; // Array to store pixel values
  struct Image* next;               // Pointer to the next image in the linked list
} Image;
```


Note that we use the `unsigned char` type to store the bytes of the image. This type is commonly used when dealing with raw binary data or when you need to ensure that values are treated as non-negative.

The struct also contains a pointer to another `Image` struct, which will be used to create a *linked list* to store all the images.

Next, we define a function that will calculate the *Euclidean distance* between two images:

```c
// Calculate Euclidean distance between two images
double euclideanDistance(Image* img1, Image* img2)
{
  double distance = 0.0;
  for (int i = 0; i < IMAGE_SIZE; i++)
  {
    distance += sqrt(pow((img1->pixels[i] - img2->pixels[i]), 2));
  }
  return sqrt(distance);
}
```


We are essentially calculating the sum of the differences between the respective bytes of two images. If the images are similar in content, then the distance will be minimized. Conversely, the distance will be higher, for images that have significant differences.

Now, we define the function to insert a new `Image` node into the linked list:

```c
// Insert a new image into the linked list
void insertImage(Image** head, unsigned char pixels[])
{
  Image* newImage = (Image*)malloc(sizeof(Image));
  if (newImage == NULL)
  {
    printf("Memory allocation failed.\n");
    exit(EXIT_FAILURE);
  }
  for (int i = 0; i < IMAGE_SIZE; i++)
  {
    newImage->pixels[i] = pixels[i];
  }
```

```c
  newImage->next = *head;
  *head = newImage;
}
```

Listing 17-3: MNISTImages.c

We allocate memory for a new Image object, and we copy the image contents into the object's array. Then, we insert to node at the beginning of the linked list.

We also define a function to free all the allocated memory in the linked list:

```c
// Free memory allocated for the linked list
void freeList(Image* head)
{
  Image* temp;
  while (head != NULL)
  {
    temp = head;
    head = head->next;
    free(temp);
  }
}
```

Listing 17-4: MNISTImages.c

Next, we define a function that will get us a randomly selected image from the linked list:

```c
// Get a random image from the linked list
Image* getRandomImage(Image* head)
{
  int length = 0;
  Image* current = head;
  while (current != NULL)
  {
    length++;
    current = current->next;
  }
  if (length == 0)
  {
    printf("Empty list.\n");
    return NULL;
  }

  // Seed the random number generator
  srand(time(NULL));

  // Generate a random index within the range of the list length
  int randomIndex = rand() % length;
  printf("Random index: %d\n", randomIndex);

  // Traverse the list to the randomly chosen index
  current = head;
  for (int i = 0; i < randomIndex; i++)
  {
```

```c
    current = current->next;
  }

  return current;
}
```


Now, let's see the `main()` function:

```c
int main()
{
  FILE* file;
  int pixels[IMAGE_SIZE];
  Image* head = NULL;
  Image* tail = NULL;

  // Open the file
  file = fopen("input.dat", "rb"); // Open in binary mode to read exact bytes
  if (file == NULL)
  {
    printf("Error opening file.\n");
    exit(EXIT_FAILURE);
  }

  // Skip the meta data at the beginning of the file
  fseek(file, META_DATA_SIZE, SEEK_SET);

  int count = 0;
  // Read data from the file and insert images into the linked list
  while (fread(pixels, sizeof(unsigned char), IMAGE_SIZE, file) == IMAGE_SIZE)
  {
    insertImage(&head, pixels);
    if (ftell(file) % (IMAGE_SIZE * IMAGE_SIZE * sizeof(int)) == 0)
    {
      tail = head;
      while (tail->next != NULL)
      {
        tail = tail->next;
      }
    }
    count++;
  }

  printf("Total images: %d\n", count);

  fclose(file);

  // Example: Find the closest image to a randomly selected image
  Image* randomImage = getRandomImage(head); // Implement this function accordingly

  // Print selected image
  for (int i = 0; i < 28; i++)
  {
    for (int j = 0; j < 28; j++)
```

```c
    {
      if (randomImage->pixels[28 * i + j] == 0)
        printf(" ");
      else
        printf("*");
    }
    printf("\n");
  }

  Image* closestImage = NULL;
  double minDistance = INFINITY;
  Image* current = head;
  int index = 0, minIndex = 0;

  while (current != NULL)
  {
    double distance = euclideanDistance(randomImage, current);
    if (distance != 0 && distance < minDistance)
    {
      minDistance = distance;
      minIndex = index;
      closestImage = current;
    }
    current = current->next;
    index++;
  }

  // Output the label of the closest image
  printf("Closest image (distance=%f, index=%d)\n", minDistance, minIndex);

  // Print closest image
  for (int i = 0; i < 28; i++)
  {
    for (int j = 0; j < 28; j++)
    {
      if (closestImage->pixels[28 * i + j] == 0)
        printf(" ");
      else
        printf("*");
    }
    printf("\n");
  }

  // Free memory allocated for the linked list
  freeList(head);

  return 0;
}
```


After we open the *input.dat* binary file, we skip the first 15 bytes with `fseek()`. Then, in a loop, we read one image at a time (784 bytes) with `fread()` and we add the respective `Image` object into the linked list.

Afterwards, we get a randomly selected image from the list and we print it using empty space where the byte is zero and an asterisk ('*') in places where the image bytes are non-zero. This way, we can get an idea of the handwriting digit that was chosen:

After printing the selected image, we iterate the whole linked list, and we calculate the Euclidian distance between the randomly selected image and the currently selected image from the list. We maintain the minimum distance encountered and the corresponding image along with its ID.

At the end, we print the closest image that we got; it seems that the algorithm is working fine.

As a final note, this algorithm will take a lot of time to get the closest image, as it is checking all the images, one by one. There are other algorithms that will make this operation faster, albeit, with a loss of precision.

One such example is the Locality-Sensitive Hashing[2] (LSH) algorithm, a technique used for approximate nearest neighbor search in high-dimensional spaces. LSH is particularly useful when dealing with large datasets where traditional exact nearest neighbor search methods become computationally expensive.

You can find this project in GitHub:

https://github.com/htset/advanced_c_exercises/tree/master/MNISTImages

---

[2] https://en.wikipedia.org/wiki/Locality-sensitive_hashing

18. HTTP Server with Caching

In this exercise, we will create a simple HTTP server that will serve static content (only HTML files). The web server will make use of a cache mechanism that will keep the most recently served content, in order to boost the server's performance.

The web server cache is a structure that stores the content that was previously sent to the client browser. The cache has limited space, so when it is filled up, we will need to empty the *least recently used (LRU)* entry in order to make space for the new entry. Moreover, when an entry is used by the server to send content to the client, then this entry is moved to the head of the list, as it is the more recently used entry.

Let's see the cache definition:

```c
#include <stdio.h>
#include <stdlib.h>
#include <string.h>
#include <winsock2.h>

#define PORT 8080
#define MAX_REQUEST_SIZE 1024
#define CACHE_SIZE 3

#pragma comment(lib, "ws2_32.lib")

// Node structure for doubly linked list
typedef struct Node
{
    char* url;
    char* content;
    struct Node* prev;
    struct Node* next;
} Node;

// Cache structure
typedef struct LRUCache
{
    int capacity;
    int size;
    Node* head;
    Node* tail;
} LRUCache;

LRUCache* cache;

Node* createNode(char* url, char* content);
void deleteNode(Node* node);
void insertAtHead(Node* node);
void moveToHead(Node* node);
char* getContent(char* url);
```

```
void putContent(char* url, char* content);
void handleRequest(SOCKET clientSocket);
```


The cache is implemented as a *doubly linked list*. In this kind of linked list, we can move to both directions, forward and backward. The doubly linked list is beneficial in our case as we can efficiently remove and insert nodes anywhere in the list without needing to traverse the list from the beginning. The same effect could be achieved with simple linked lists, or even arrays, but with lower performance.

Also, note this line:

```
#pragma comment(lib, "ws2_32.lib")
```

It instructs the linker to add the ws2_32.lib library to the list of library dependencies. This is alternative to adding it in the project properties at *Linker->Input->Additional dependencies*.

Next, we have the `main()` function of our program:

```c
int main()
{
  WSADATA wsaData;
  SOCKET listenSocket, clientSocket;
  struct sockaddr_in serverAddr, clientAddr;
  int addrLen = sizeof(struct sockaddr_in);

  // Initialize Winsock
  if (WSAStartup(MAKEWORD(2, 2), &wsaData) != 0)
  {
    perror("WSAStartup");
    return 1;
  }

  // Create socket
  if ((listenSocket = socket(AF_INET, SOCK_STREAM, 0)) == INVALID_SOCKET)
  {
    perror("socket");
    return 1;
  }

  // Initialize server address
  memset(&serverAddr, 0, sizeof(serverAddr));
  serverAddr.sin_family = AF_INET;
  serverAddr.sin_addr.s_addr = INADDR_ANY;
  serverAddr.sin_port = htons(PORT);

  // Bind socket to address
  if (bind(listenSocket, (struct sockaddr*)&serverAddr,
    sizeof(serverAddr)) == SOCKET_ERROR)
  {
```

```c
  perror("bind");
  closesocket(listenSocket);
  WSACleanup();
  return 1;
}

// Listen for connections
if (listen(listenSocket, SOMAXCONN) == SOCKET_ERROR)
{
  perror("listen");
  closesocket(listenSocket);
  WSACleanup();
  return 1;
}

// Initialize cache
cache = (LRUCache*)malloc(sizeof(LRUCache));
cache->capacity = CACHE_SIZE;
cache->size = 0;
cache->head = NULL;
cache->tail = NULL;

printf("Server started on port %d...\n", PORT);

while (1)
{
  // Accept connections
  if ((clientSocket = accept(listenSocket,
    (struct sockaddr*)&clientAddr, &addrLen)) == INVALID_SOCKET)
  {
    perror("accept");
    continue;
  }

  printf("Connection from %s\n", inet_ntoa(clientAddr.sin_addr));

  // Handle client request
  handleRequest(clientSocket);

  // Close client socket
  closesocket(clientSocket);
}

// Free cache memory
Node* current = cache->head;
while (current != NULL)
{
  Node* temp = current;
  current = current->next;
  deleteNode(temp);
}
free(cache);

// Close server socket
```

```c
    closesocket(listenSocket);

    // Cleanup Winsock
    WSACleanup();

    return 0;
}
```


Here we create a server socket that continuously accepts HTTP connections from web browsers at port 8080. When a connection is accepted, then `handleRequest()` is called:

```c
void handleRequest(SOCKET clientSocket)
{
  char request[MAX_REQUEST_SIZE];
  int bytesReceived = recv(clientSocket, request, sizeof(request), 0);
  if (bytesReceived <= 0)
  {
    perror("recv");
    return;
  }
  request[bytesReceived] = '\0';

  char* url = strtok(request, " ");
  if (strcmp(url, "GET") != 0)
  {
    perror("Only GET requests are supported.");
    return;
  }

  url = strtok(NULL, " ");
  if (url == NULL)
  {
    perror("Invalid request format.");
    return;
  }

  char* content = getContent(url);
  if (content == NULL)
  {
    // Serve the page from disk
    FILE* file = fopen(url + 1, "r");
    if (file == NULL)
    {
      // File not found, return 404 response
      char response[] = "HTTP/1.1 404 Not Found\n\n";
      printf("File not found: %s\n", url + 1);
      send(clientSocket, response, strlen(response), 0);
      return;
    }

    char response[MAX_REQUEST_SIZE];
    snprintf(response, sizeof(response),
```

```c
    "HTTP/1.1 200 OK\nContent-Type: text/html\n\n");
    send(clientSocket, response, strlen(response), 0);

    char buffer[MAX_REQUEST_SIZE];
    while (fgets(buffer, sizeof(buffer), file) != NULL)
    {
      send(clientSocket, buffer, strlen(buffer), 0);
    }
    fclose(file);
    printf("Got content from file: %s\n", buffer);

    // Cache the page content
    putContent(url, buffer);
  }
  else
  {
    // Serve the page from cache
    char response[MAX_REQUEST_SIZE];
    snprintf(response, sizeof(response),
      "HTTP/1.1 200 OK\nContent-Type: text/html\n\n");
    send(clientSocket, response, strlen(response), 0);

    send(clientSocket, content, strlen(content), 0);
  }
}
```


Initially, the web request is received into the `request` buffer. We make sure that the last character of the input contains the string null termination. Then we use the `strtok()` tokenizing function to get the request type and URL; only GET requests are handled by our server.

We then use the request URL to search in the cache for a previously stored response for this URL. If such an entry is not found in the cache, then we open the requested HTML file (The HTML files are stored in the same folder as our executable) and we transmit its HTML content in the response. Note that, before sending the content, we send the header of the response:

```
HTTP/1.1 200 OK\nContent-Type: text/html
```

If the URL is found in the cache, then we get the content from there and we send it with the response.

Let's see how we do this, in function `getContent()`:

```c
// Get the content associated with a URL from the cache
char* getContent(char* url)
{
  Node* current = cache->head;
  while (current != NULL)
  {
```

```c
    if (strcmp(current->url, url) == 0)
    {
      moveToHead(current);
      printf("Got content from cache: %s\n", current->content);

      return current->content;
    }
    current = current->next;
  }
  // Return NULL if the URL is not found in cache
  return NULL;
}
```


We start from the head of the list, and we search for the URL in the cache's nodes. If we find the URL, then we move the node to the head of the cache (the *most recently used entry*) and we return the stored HTML content. The function returns NULL if the URL is not found in the cache.

When a page is read from its file, then we store its content into the cache, with putContent():

```c
// Put a URL-content pair into the cache
void putContent(char* url, char* content)
{
  if (cache->size == CACHE_SIZE)
  {
    deleteNode(cache->tail);
    cache->size--;
  }
  Node* newNode = createNode(url, content);
  insertAtHead(newNode);
  cache->size++;
}
```


If we have reached the maximum cache size, then the *LRU algorithm* kicks in: we delete the least recently used entry (the node at the tail of the list) and we make space for the insertion of the new entry (at the head of the list).

Now we can examine the functions that handle the cache operations. First, let's see how we can create a new node:

```c
// Create a new node
Node* createNode(char* url, char* content)
{
  Node* newNode = (Node*)malloc(sizeof(Node));
  newNode->url = _strdup(url);
  newNode->content = _strdup(content);
  newNode->prev = NULL;
  newNode->next = NULL;
```

```c
    printf("New node created: %s\n", content);
    return newNode;
}
```


Next, we see how to insert a new node at the head of the cache:

```c
// Insert a new node at the head of the cache
void insertAtHead(Node* node)
{
    node->next = cache->head;
    node->prev = NULL;
    if (cache->head != NULL)
    {
        cache->head->prev = node;
    }
    cache->head = node;
    if (cache->tail == NULL)
    {
        cache->tail = node;
    }
    printf("Node inserted at head: %s\n", node->content);
}
```


Note that in all operations we have to take care of all four pointers: head, tail, next, prev.

As part of the LRU algorithm, we have to move a node to the head of the list:

```c
// Move a node to the head of the cache
void moveToHead(Node* node)
{
    if (node == cache->head)
    {
        // Node is already at the head, no need to move
        return;
    }

    // Adjust pointers to remove node from its current position
    if (node->prev != NULL)
    {
        node->prev->next = node->next;
    }
    if (node->next != NULL)
    {
        node->next->prev = node->prev;
    }

    // Update pointers to insert node at the head
    node->prev = NULL;
    node->next = cache->head;
    if (cache->head != NULL)
    {
```

```c
    cache->head->prev = node;
  }
  cache->head = node;
  if (cache->tail == NULL)
  {
    cache->tail = node;
  }
  printf("Node moved to head: %s\n", node->content);
}
```


Finally, here is the code for node deletion:

```c
// Delete a node from the cache
void deleteNode(Node* node)
{
  if (node == NULL)
    return;

  // If the node is the head of the list
  if (node == cache->head)
  {
    cache->head = node->next;
  }

  // If the node is the tail of the list
  if (node == cache->tail)
  {
    cache->tail = node->prev;
  }

  // Adjust pointers of neighboring nodes
  if (node->prev != NULL)
  {
    node->prev->next = node->next;
  }
  if (node->next != NULL)
  {
    node->next->prev = node->prev;
  }
  printf("Node deleted: %s\n", node->content);

  free(node->url);
  free(node->content);
  free(node);
}
```


We make sure to release the memory that was used for this node, in order to avoid memory leaks.

Here is the same code for Linux:

```c
#include <stdio.h>
#include <stdlib.h>
#include <string.h>
#include <sys/socket.h>
#include <netinet/in.h>
#include <unistd.h>
#include <errno.h>

#define PORT 8080
#define MAX_REQUEST_SIZE 1024
#define CACHE_SIZE 3

// Node structure for doubly linked list
typedef struct Node
{
    char *url;
    char *content;
    struct Node *prev;
    struct Node *next;
} Node;

// Cache structure
typedef struct LRUCache
{
    int capacity;
    int size;
    Node *head;
    Node *tail;
} LRUCache;

LRUCache *cache;

Node *createNode(char *url, char *content);
void deleteNode(Node *node);
void insertAtHead(Node *node);
void moveToHead(Node *node);
char *getContent(char *url);
void putContent(char *url, char *content);
void handleRequest(int clientSocket);

int main()
{
    int serverSocket, clientSocket;
    struct sockaddr_in serverAddr, clientAddr;
    socklen_t addrSize;

    // Create socket
    serverSocket = socket(AF_INET, SOCK_STREAM, 0);
    if (serverSocket < 0)
    {
        perror("Socket creation failed");
```

```c
    return errno;
  }

  // Bind socket
  serverAddr.sin_family = AF_INET;
  serverAddr.sin_addr.s_addr = INADDR_ANY;
  serverAddr.sin_port = htons(PORT);
  if (bind(serverSocket, (struct sockaddr *)&serverAddr, sizeof(serverAddr)) < 0)
  {
    perror("Socket binding failed");
    return errno;
  }

  // Listen for connections
  if (listen(serverSocket, 5) < 0)
  {
    perror("Listen failed");
    return errno;
  }

  // Initialize cache
  cache = (LRUCache *)malloc(sizeof(LRUCache));
  cache->capacity = CACHE_SIZE;
  cache->size = 0;
  cache->head = NULL;
  cache->tail = NULL;

  printf("Server listening on port %d\n", PORT);

  while (1)
  {
    addrSize = sizeof(clientAddr);
    // Accept incoming connection
    clientSocket = accept(serverSocket, (struct sockaddr *)&clientAddr, &addrSize);
    if (clientSocket < 0)
    {
      perror("Accept failed");
      return errno;
    }

    // Convert client IP address and port to printable format
    char clientIP[INET_ADDRSTRLEN];
    inet_ntop(AF_INET, &(clientAddr.sin_addr), clientIP, INET_ADDRSTRLEN);

    // Print connection information
    printf("Connection accepted from %s:%d\n", clientIP, ntohs(clientAddr.sin_port));

    // Handle client request
    handleRequest(clientSocket);

    // Close client socket
    close(clientSocket);
  }
```

```c
  // Close server socket
  close(serverSocket);

  return 0;
}

void handleRequest(int clientSocket)
{
  char request[MAX_REQUEST_SIZE];
  int bytesReceived = recv(clientSocket, request, sizeof(request), 0);
  if (bytesReceived <= 0)
  {
    perror("recv");
    return;
  }
  request[bytesReceived] = '\0';

  char *url = strtok(request, " ");
  if (strcmp(url, "GET") != 0)
  {
    perror("Only GET requests are supported.");
    return;
  }

  url = strtok(NULL, " ");
  if (url == NULL)
  {
    perror("Invalid request format.");
    return;
  }

  char *content = getContent(url);
  if (content == NULL)
  {
    // Serve the page from disk
    FILE *file = fopen(url + 1, "r");
    if (file == NULL)
    {
      // File not found, return 404 response
      char response[] = "HTTP/1.1 404 Not Found\n\n";
      printf("File not found: %s\n", url + 1);
      send(clientSocket, response, strlen(response), 0);
      return;
    }

    char response[MAX_REQUEST_SIZE];
    snprintf(response, sizeof(response),
            "HTTP/1.1 200 OK\nContent-Type: text/html\n\n");
    send(clientSocket, response, strlen(response), 0);

    char buffer[MAX_REQUEST_SIZE];
    while (fgets(buffer, sizeof(buffer), file) != NULL)
    {
      send(clientSocket, buffer, strlen(buffer), 0);
```

```c
        }
        fclose(file);
        printf("Got content from file: %s\n", buffer);

        // Cache the page content
        putContent(url, buffer);
    }
    else
    {
        // Serve the page from cache
        char response[MAX_REQUEST_SIZE];
        snprintf(response, sizeof(response),
                 "HTTP/1.1 200 OK\nContent-Type: text/html\n\n");
        send(clientSocket, response, strlen(response), 0);

        send(clientSocket, content, strlen(content), 0);
    }
}

// Get the content associated with a URL from the cache
char *getContent(char *url)
{
    Node *current = cache->head;
    while (current != NULL)
    {
        if (strcmp(current->url, url) == 0)
        {
            moveToHead(current);
            printf("Got content from cache: %s\n", current->content);

            return current->content;
        }
        current = current->next;
    }
    // Return NULL if the URL is not found in cache
    return NULL;
}

// Put a URL-content pair into the cache
void putContent(char *url, char *content)
{
    if (cache->size == CACHE_SIZE)
    {
        deleteNode(cache->tail);
        cache->size--;
    }
    Node *newNode = createNode(url, content);
    insertAtHead(newNode);
    cache->size++;
}

// Create a new node
Node *createNode(char *url, char *content)
{
```

```c
  Node *newNode = (Node *)malloc(sizeof(Node));
  newNode->url = strdup(url);
  newNode->content = strdup(content);
  newNode->prev = NULL;
  newNode->next = NULL;
  printf("New node created: %s\n", content);
  return newNode;
}

// Insert a new node at the head of the cache
void insertAtHead(Node *node)
{
  node->next = cache->head;
  node->prev = NULL;
  if (cache->head != NULL)
  {
    cache->head->prev = node;
  }
  cache->head = node;
  if (cache->tail == NULL)
  {
    cache->tail = node;
  }
  printf("Node inserted at head: %s\n", node->content);
}

// Move a node to the head of the cache
void moveToHead(Node *node)
{
  if (node == cache->head)
  {
    // Node is already at the head, no need to move
    return;
  }

  // Adjust pointers to remove node from its current position
  if (node->prev != NULL)
  {
    node->prev->next = node->next;
  }
  if (node->next != NULL)
  {
    node->next->prev = node->prev;
  }

  // Update pointers to insert node at the head
  node->prev = NULL;
  node->next = cache->head;
  if (cache->head != NULL)
  {
    cache->head->prev = node;
  }
  cache->head = node;
  if (cache->tail == NULL)
```

```c
  {
    cache->tail = node;
  }
  printf("Node moved to head: %s\n", node->content);
}

// Delete a node from the cache
void deleteNode(Node *node)
{
  if (node == NULL)
    return;

  // If the node is the head of the list
  if (node == cache->head)
  {
    cache->head = node->next;
  }

  // If the node is the tail of the list
  if (node == cache->tail)
  {
    cache->tail = node->prev;
  }

  // Adjust pointers of neighboring nodes
  if (node->prev != NULL)
  {
    node->prev->next = node->next;
  }
  if (node->next != NULL)
  {
    node->next->prev = node->prev;
  }
  printf("Node deleted: %s\n", node->content);

  free(node->url);
  free(node->content);
  free(node);
}
```


We have changed only the code inside the `main()` function so that we can use Linux sockets. A couple more adaptations have been made, outside `main()`; they are underlined in the code snippet.

You can find this project in GitHub:

https://github.com/htset/advanced_c_exercises/tree/master/WebServerCache

https://github.com/htset/advanced_c_exercises/tree/master/WebServerCacheLinux

19. Distributed Auction

In this exercise, we will create a distributed auction, that will consist of an auction server that receives bids from multiple clients. The clients will communicate with the server via sockets. The server will wait for 20 seconds (using a timer) for a new bid, or else the auction is over and the maximum bid wins. The timer will be reset upon timely submission of new bid.

Proposed Solution (Windows)

Let's start wih the auction server. The server should be able to accommodate multiple clients. For this reason, each client will be served in a separate *thread*, that will be spawned when the server socket accepts a new connection:

```c
#include <stdio.h>
#include <winsock2.h>
#include <windows.h>
#include <process.h>

#pragma comment(lib, "ws2_32.lib")

#define PORT 8080
#define MAX_CLIENTS 5

// Structure to hold client information
typedef struct
{
    SOCKET socket;
    struct sockaddr_in address;
    int addr_len;
    int id;
} Client;

// Global variables for bid information
Client clients[MAX_CLIENTS];
HANDLE timer;
SOCKET server_socket;
int best_bid = 0;
int winning_client = 0;

VOID CALLBACK TimerCompletionRoutine(PVOID lpParam, BOOLEAN TimerOrWaitFired);
unsigned __stdcall client_handler(void* data);
```


Here we define the `Client` struct that stores information about the connected client. We also define global variables, as well as the signature of two callback functions that will be implemented below.

Next, we have the `main()` function:

```c
int main()
```

```c
{
  WSADATA wsa;
  struct sockaddr_in server_addr;
  int addr_len = sizeof(server_addr);

  // Initialize Winsock
  if (WSAStartup(MAKEWORD(2, 2), &wsa) != 0)
  {
    printf("WSAStartup failed.\n");
    return 1;
  }

  // Create server socket
  if ((server_socket = socket(AF_INET, SOCK_STREAM, 0)) == INVALID_SOCKET)
  {
    printf("Socket creation failed.\n");
    return 1;
  }

  // Prepare the sockaddr_in struct
  server_addr.sin_family = AF_INET;
  server_addr.sin_addr.s_addr = INADDR_ANY;
  server_addr.sin_port = htons(PORT);

  // Bind server socket
  if (bind(server_socket, (struct sockaddr*)&server_addr, sizeof(server_addr)) ==
SOCKET_ERROR)
  {
    printf("Bind failed with error: %d\n", WSAGetLastError());
    return 1;
  }

  // Listen to server socket
  if (listen(server_socket, 5) == SOCKET_ERROR)
  {
    printf("Listen failed with error: %d\n", WSAGetLastError());
    return 1;
  }
  printf("Server listening on port %d\n", PORT);

  // Create a waitable timer
  timer = CreateWaitableTimer(NULL, TRUE, NULL);
  LARGE_INTEGER dueTime;
  dueTime.QuadPart = -200000000LL; // 20 seconds
  SetWaitableTimer(timer, &dueTime, 0, TimerCompletionRoutine, NULL, 0);

  while (1)
  {
    // Accept incoming connections and handle each client
    SOCKET client_socket;
    Client client;
    client.addr_len = sizeof(client.address);

    // Accept connection from client
```

```c
    if ((client_socket = accept(server_socket,
        (struct sockaddr*)&client.address, &client.addr_len)) == INVALID_SOCKET)
    {
        printf("Accept failed with error: %d\n", WSAGetLastError());
        continue;
    }

    // Add client to the clients array
    int c = 0;
    for (int i = 0; i < MAX_CLIENTS; i++)
    {
        if (clients[i].socket == 0)
        {
            clients[i].socket = client_socket;
            clients[i].address = client.address;
            clients[i].addr_len = client.addr_len;
            clients[i].id = i + 1;
            c = i;
            printf("Client no.%d connected.\n", i+1);
            break;
        }
    }

    // Handle client in a separate thread
    _beginthreadex(NULL, 0, client_handler, &clients[c], 0, NULL);
    }
    return 0;
}
```


After initializing the Winsock library, we open a new *server socket*, and we listen for new connections. When a new connection arrives, we store the client details in an array and we spawn a new thread with _beginthreadex().

As an argument to this function we pass the address of the client_handler() callback function, that will handle the communication with the specific client.

Note also, that we create a *WaitableTimer* object. We set its due time to 20 seconds and we supply as argument the address of the other callback function, TimerCompletionRoutine(). This function will be called back when the timer expires, in order to handle the auction expiration event.

Now, let's see the first of the callback functions:

```c
// Callback function to handle client connection
unsigned __stdcall client_handler(void* data)
{
  Client* client = (Client*)data;
  SOCKET client_socket = client->socket;
  char buffer[1024] = { 0 };
  int bid_amount;
```

```c
while (1)
{
  // Receive bid amount from client
  int valread = recv(client_socket, buffer, sizeof(buffer), 0);
  if (valread <= 0)
  {
    if (valread == 0)
      printf("Client disconnected.\n");
    else
      printf("Recv failed with error: %d\n", WSAGetLastError());

    break;
  }
  bid_amount = atoi(buffer);
  printf("Received bid $%d from client %d\n", bid_amount, client->id);

  // Update best bid if necessary
  if (bid_amount > best_bid)
  {
    best_bid = bid_amount;
    winning_client = client->id;

    // Inform all clients about the new best bid
    char msg[1024];
    sprintf(msg, "New best bid: $%d (Client: %d)", best_bid, winning_client);
    for (int i = 0; i < MAX_CLIENTS; i++)
    {
      if (clients[i].socket != 0)
      {
        send(clients[i].socket, msg, strlen(msg), 0);
      }
    }

    // Restart the timer
    LARGE_INTEGER dueTime;
    dueTime.QuadPart = -200000000LL; // 10 seconds in 100-nanosecond intervals
    SetWaitableTimer(timer, &dueTime, 0, TimerCompletionRoutine, NULL, 0);
  }
  else
  {
    char msg[1024];
    sprintf(msg, "Received lower bid. Best bid remains at: $%d", best_bid);
    for (int i = 0; i < MAX_CLIENTS; i++)
    {
      if (clients[i].socket != 0)
      {
        send(clients[i].socket, msg, strlen(msg), 0);
      }
    }
  }
}
return 0;
}
```

Function `client_handler()` takes care of the communication with the client. This function gets as input a pointer to the `Client` struct, that was passed in `main()`:

```c
_beginthreadex(NULL, 0, client_handler, &clients[c], 0, NULL);
```

Then, in an endless while loop, it blocks in the `resv()` function, waiting for input from the client. When a message arrives, the function is unblocked and continues to check the input. If the number of bytes read is 0, the client has disconnected. If it is equal to -1, then there was an error with the connection.

If the client has actually sent a valid bid, we compare it with the current maximum bid and we update this value if we got a higher bid. We also proceed with informing all clients about the submitted bid.

We also reset the timer to get a new 20 seconds' period. We achieve this by setting the timer again.

When the timer eventually expires, the `TimerCompletionRoutine()` function will be called:

```c
// Callback function to finish the auction after 20 seconds of inactivity
VOID CALLBACK TimerCompletionRoutine(PVOID lpParam, BOOLEAN TimerOrWaitFired)
{
  printf("Auction finished. Winning bid: $%d, winner: client no. %d\n", best_bid,
winning_client);

  // Inform all clients about the end of the auction
  char msg[1024];
  sprintf(msg, "Auction finished. Winning bid: $%d, winner: client no. %d",
    best_bid, winning_client);
  for (int i = 0; i < MAX_CLIENTS; i++)
  {
    if (clients[i].socket != 0)
    {
      send(clients[i].socket, msg, strlen(msg), 0);
    }
  }

  CloseHandle(timer);
  closesocket(server_socket);
  WSACleanup();

  exit(EXIT_SUCCESS);
}
```


After informing all clients about the winning bid, we close the timer handle and the server socket. After performing a cleanup of Winsock, we exit the program. The client sockets will be closed by the respective clients when they receive the message of the auction completion.

__stdcall is the calling convention used for the function. This tells the compiler the rules that apply for setting up the stack, pushing arguments and getting a return value.

Now for the auction client, we first implement the main() function:

```c
#include <stdio.h>
#include <stdlib.h>
#include <string.h>
#include <winsock2.h>
#include <windows.h>
#include <process.h>

#pragma comment(lib, "ws2_32.lib")

#define PORT 8080
#define SERVER_IP "127.0.0.1"

SOCKET client_socket;
int is_running = 1;
HANDLE receive_thread;

unsigned __stdcall receive_handler(void* arg);

int main()
{
  WSADATA wsa;
  struct sockaddr_in server_addr;
  int addr_len = sizeof(server_addr);

  // Initialize Winsock
  if (WSAStartup(MAKEWORD(2, 2), &wsa) != 0)
  {
    printf("WSAStartup failed.\n");
    return 1;
  }

  // Create socket
  if ((client_socket = socket(AF_INET, SOCK_STREAM, 0)) == INVALID_SOCKET)
  {
    printf("Socket creation failed.\n");
    return 1;
  }

  server_addr.sin_family = AF_INET;
  server_addr.sin_port = htons(PORT);

  if (inet_pton(AF_INET, SERVER_IP, &server_addr.sin_addr) <= 0)
  {
    perror("inet_pton");
    closesocket(client_socket);
    WSACleanup();
```

```c
        return 1;
    }

    if (connect(client_socket, (struct sockaddr*)&server_addr, sizeof(server_addr)) ==
SOCKET_ERROR)
    {
        printf("Connect failed.\n");
        closesocket(client_socket);
        WSACleanup();
        return 1;
    }

    printf("Connected to server.\n");

    receive_thread = (HANDLE)_beginthreadex(NULL, 0, receive_handler, NULL, 0, NULL);
    if (receive_thread == NULL)
    {
        perror("_beginthreadex");
        closesocket(client_socket);
        WSACleanup();
        return 1;
    }

    char buffer[1024];
    while (is_running)
    {
        printf("\nEnter your bid (or 'q' to quit): ");
        fgets(buffer, sizeof(buffer), stdin);
        buffer[strcspn(buffer, "\n")] = '\0'; // Remove newline character

        if (strcmp(buffer, "q") == 0)
        {
            break;
        }

        if (send(client_socket, buffer, strlen(buffer), 0) == SOCKET_ERROR)
        {
            printf("Send failed.\n");
            closesocket(client_socket);
            WSACleanup();
            return 1;
        }
    }

    return 0;
}
```

Listing 19-5: auctionClient.c

Here, we create a client socket, and we connect to the server. If the connection is successful, we spawn a new thread that will be used to receive and print the information from the server.

The sending part of the communication, i.e. the submission of bids to the server, will be performed by the main thread. If we had the same thread handle sending and receiving of data, we would have a problem, as the `recv()` function would block and would not let the user send a new bid.

Here is the callback function for the thread handler:

```c
unsigned __stdcall receive_handler(void* arg)
{
  char buffer[1024] = { 0 };
  while (1)
  {
    int valread = recv(client_socket, buffer, sizeof(buffer), 0);
    if (valread <= 0)
    {
      if (valread == 0)
        printf("\nServer disconnected.\n");
      else
        perror("recv");
      }
      break;
    }

    printf("\nServer: %s\n", buffer);
    if (strncmp(buffer, "Auction", 7) == 0)
    {
      printf("Auction ended. Exiting program.\n");

      CloseHandle(receive_thread);
      closesocket(client_socket);
      WSACleanup();

      exit(EXIT_SUCCESS);
    }

    memset(buffer, 0, sizeof(buffer));
    printf("\nEnter your bid (or 'q' to quit): ");
  }
  return 0;
}
```

Listing 19-6: auctionClient.c

This thread receives messages from the auction server and prints them in console. When the final message, starting with "Auction" arrives, then it closes down the resources and exits the program.

Here is the code for the auction server:

```c
#include <stdio.h>
#include <stdlib.h>
#include <string.h>
#include <unistd.h>
#include <netinet/in.h>
#include <sys/socket.h>
#include <pthread.h>
#include <time.h>

#define PORT 8080
#define MAX_CLIENTS 5

typedef struct
{
  int socket;
  struct sockaddr_in address;
  int addr_len;
  int id;
} Client;

Client clients[MAX_CLIENTS];
int server_socket;
int best_bid = 0;
int winning_client = 0;
pthread_mutex_t mutex = PTHREAD_MUTEX_INITIALIZER;
time_t last_bid_time;

void *timer_thread(void *arg);
void *client_handler(void *arg);

int main()
{
  struct sockaddr_in server_addr, client_addr;
  socklen_t client_addr_len = sizeof(client_addr);
  pthread_t threads[MAX_CLIENTS];
  pthread_t timer;
  time(&last_bid_time);

  // Create server socket
  if ((server_socket = socket(AF_INET, SOCK_STREAM, 0)) == -1)
  {
    perror("Socket creation failed");
    exit(EXIT_FAILURE);
  }

  // Bind server socket
  server_addr.sin_family = AF_INET;
  server_addr.sin_addr.s_addr = INADDR_ANY;
  server_addr.sin_port = htons(PORT);
  if (bind(server_socket, (struct sockaddr *)&server_addr, sizeof(server_addr)) == -
1)
  {
```

```c
      perror("Bind failed");
      close(server_socket);
      exit(EXIT_FAILURE);
  }

  // Listen for incoming connections
  if (listen(server_socket, MAX_CLIENTS) == -1)
  {
    perror("Listen failed");
    close(server_socket);
    exit(EXIT_FAILURE);
  }

  printf("Server listening on port %d...\n", PORT);

  // Create thread for timer
  if (pthread_create(&timer, NULL, timer_thread, NULL) != 0)
  {
    perror("Timer thread creation failed");
    close(server_socket);
    exit(EXIT_FAILURE);
  }

  while (1)
  {
    int client_socket;
    Client client;

    // Accept incoming connection
    client_socket = accept(server_socket, (struct sockaddr *)&client_addr,
&client_addr_len);
    if (client_socket == -1)
    {
      perror("Accept failed");
      close(server_socket);
      exit(EXIT_FAILURE);
    }

    // Add client to the clients array
    int c = 0;
    for (int i = 0; i < MAX_CLIENTS; i++)
    {
      if (clients[i].socket == 0)
      {
        clients[i].socket = client_socket;
        clients[i].address = client.address;
        clients[i].addr_len = client.addr_len;
        clients[i].id = i + 1;
        c = i;
        printf("Client no.%d connected.\n", i+1);
        break;
      }
    }
```

```c
    if (pthread_create(&threads[c], NULL, client_handler, (void *)&clients[c]) != 0)
    {
      perror("Thread creation failed");
      close(server_socket);
      exit(EXIT_FAILURE);
    }
  }

  close(server_socket);

  return 0;
}


void *client_handler(void *arg)
{
  Client *client = (Client *)arg;
  int client_socket = client->socket;
  char buffer[1024] = {0};
  int bid_amount;

  while (1)
  {
    // Receive bid from client
    ssize_t bytes_received = recv(client_socket, buffer, sizeof(buffer), 0);
    if (bytes_received == -1)
    {
      perror("Receive failed");
      break;
    }
    else if (bytes_received == 0)
    {
      printf("Client disconnected.\n");
      break;
    }

    pthread_mutex_lock(&mutex);
    bid_amount = atoi(buffer);
    printf("Received bid $%d from client %d\n", bid_amount, client->id);
    if (bid_amount > best_bid)
    {
      best_bid = bid_amount;
      winning_client = client->id;

      // Inform all clients about the new best bid
      char msg[1024];
      sprintf(msg, "New best bid: $%d (Client: %d)", best_bid, winning_client);
      for (int i = 0; i < MAX_CLIENTS; i++)
      {
        if (clients[i].socket != 0)
        {
          send(clients[i].socket, msg, strlen(msg), 0);
        }
      }
    }
```

```c
        time(&last_bid_time); // Update the last bid time
      }
      else
      {
        char msg[1024];
        sprintf(msg, "Received lower bid. Best bid remains at: $%d", best_bid);
        for (int i = 0; i < MAX_CLIENTS; i++)
        {
          if (clients[i].socket != 0)
          {
            send(clients[i].socket, msg, strlen(msg), 0);
          }
        }
      }

      pthread_mutex_unlock(&mutex);
  }
}


void *timer_thread(void *arg)
{
  while (1)
  {
    time_t current_time;
    time(&current_time);
    double elapsed_seconds = difftime(current_time, last_bid_time);

    if (elapsed_seconds >= 20)
    {
      pthread_mutex_lock(&mutex);
      printf("Auction ended. Maximum bid: %d\n", best_bid);

      // Inform all clients about the end of the auction
      char msg[1024];
      sprintf(msg, "Auction finished. Winning bid: $%d", best_bid);
      for (int i = 0; i < MAX_CLIENTS; i++)
      {
        if (clients[i].socket != 0)
        {
          send(clients[i].socket, msg, strlen(msg), 0);
        }
      }
      close(server_socket);

      pthread_mutex_unlock(&mutex);

      exit(0);
    }

    sleep(1);
  }

  pthread_exit(NULL);
```

}

Here we use the Unix socket functions, that are a bit different from Winsock. We also use the POSIX function `pthread_create()` to spawn a new thread.

The auction timer is implemented with sleeping for one second each time; After 20 seconds have elapsed without a new bid, the auction ends.

Here is the code for the auction client:

```c
#include <stdio.h>
#include <stdlib.h>
#include <string.h>
#include <unistd.h>
#include <arpa/inet.h>
#include <netinet/in.h>
#include <sys/socket.h>
#include <pthread.h>

#define PORT 8080
#define SERVER_IP "127.0.0.1"

int client_socket;

void *receive_handler(void *arg);

int main()
{
  struct sockaddr_in server_addr;
  pthread_t receive_thread;

  // Create client socket
  if ((client_socket = socket(AF_INET, SOCK_STREAM, 0)) == -1)
  {
    perror("Socket creation failed");
    exit(EXIT_FAILURE);
  }

  // Configure server address
  server_addr.sin_family = AF_INET;
  server_addr.sin_port = htons(PORT);
  if (inet_pton(AF_INET, SERVER_IP, &server_addr.sin_addr) <= 0)
  {
    perror("Invalid address");
    close(client_socket);
    exit(EXIT_FAILURE);
  }

  // Connect to server
  if (connect(client_socket, (struct sockaddr *)&server_addr, sizeof(server_addr)) ==
-1)
  {
```

```c
        perror("Connect failed");
        close(client_socket);
        exit(EXIT_FAILURE);
    }

    printf("Connected to server.\n");

    // Create thread to handle receiving messages from server
    if (pthread_create(&receive_thread, NULL, receive_handler, NULL) != 0)
    {
        perror("Thread creation failed");
        close(client_socket);
        exit(EXIT_FAILURE);
    }

    // Main thread to send messages to the server
    char buffer[1024];
    while (1)
    {
        printf("Enter your bid (or 'q' to quit): ");
        fgets(buffer, sizeof(buffer), stdin);
        buffer[strcspn(buffer, "\n")] = '\0'; // Remove newline character

        if (strcmp(buffer, "q") == 0)
        {
            break;
        }

        if (send(client_socket, buffer, strlen(buffer), 0) == -1)
        {
            perror("Send failed");
            close(client_socket);
            exit(EXIT_FAILURE);
        }
    }

    // Wait for the receive thread to finish
    // pthread_join(receive_thread, NULL);

    // close(client_socket);

    return 0;
}

void *receive_handler(void *arg)
{
    char buffer[1024] = {0};

    while (1)
    {
        // Receive message from server
        ssize_t bytes_received = recv(client_socket, buffer, sizeof(buffer), 0);
        if (bytes_received == -1)
        {
```

```c
      perror("Receive failed");
      break;
    }
    else if (bytes_received == 0)
    {
      printf("Server disconnected.\n");
      break;
    }

    buffer[bytes_received] = '\0';
    printf("\nServer: %s\n", buffer);

    if (strncmp(buffer, "Auction", 7) == 0)
    {
      printf("Auction ended. Exiting program.\n");

      close(client_socket);

      exit(0);
    }
    memset(buffer, 0, sizeof(buffer));
    printf("\nEnter your bid (or 'q' to quit): ");

  }

  close(client_socket);
  pthread_exit(NULL);
}
```


You can find this project in GitHub:

https://github.com/htset/advanced_c_exercises/tree/master/AuctionServer

https://github.com/htset/advanced_c_exercises/tree/master/AuctionClient

https://github.com/htset/advanced_c_exercises/tree/master/AuctionServerLinux

https://github.com/htset/advanced_c_exercises/tree/master/AuctionClientLinux